Dare
to
Ask

Wrestling from a place of rest in our pursuit of God

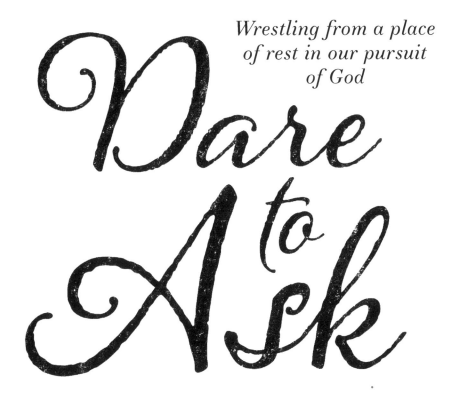

Dare to Ask

SIMCHA NATAN

What you are about to read is like a good movie with various characters, vantage points and visceral moments that are all connected by a common theme – one of great risk and great reward. I think there is something in all of us that wants to believe for great things. *Dare to Ask*, explores that belief by reintroducing a cast of biblical characters whose experiences and decisions clearly correlate with life's challenges and circumstances today.

Like a master archeologist, Simcha skillfully brushes away the dust and debris that has covered over dormant dreams so that divine destiny can be rediscovered once again – not just the destination, but the process. The revelation in the title chapter alone is well worth the price of admission, but the waves of wisdom, insight, honesty and personal application continue to roll until the very last page.

Dare to Ask challenges the resigned mindset that we are merely silent spectators in this life and beautifully reminds us that dreams are possible, miracles are real and hope is attainable if you just dare to ask.

Steve Carpenter
Founder, Highway 19 Ministries – Jerusalem

~

To the reader of *Dare to Ask*, I would say that when you reach the end of the book, you will conclude that this has been a kairos moment. It is a serendipity, a surprise discovery. Instead of it focusing on aspects of worship from a gifted worship leader, you will be taken on a moving personal journey that deepens your love for the Messiah. It leaves a lot of questions unanswered, but you are left with the deep assurance that the

Lord is in control. As readers, we are simply left to keep on asking and keep on trusting. This is a beautiful devotional book written from the heart.

Dr David Elms
International Christian Embassy Jerusalem UK Director

~

Dare To Ask has a beautiful tapestry of practicality and spirituality woven throughout the pages. It challenges readers to dream our God-given dreams, use our God-given gifts, and remove clutter from our hearts so that we can experience the fullness of what God has for us. Through her testimony and scriptural insights, Simcha demonstrates how to be grateful in all things – including trials and desert places. If you need encouragement, restoration or a fresh stirring of hope in your heart, you will find it here! Prepare to go deeper...

Michael & Sara Thorsby
Burn 24-7 New Bern, NC Directors (USA)

simchanatan.com

fb.com/simchanatan
IG: Simcha Natan

DareToAsk © Simcha Natan 2017

Cover illustration by Jo-Anna Wolstenholme © Simcha Natan

Design and layout © Jude May Design

Edited by Claire Musters

For my beautiful daughter

You were named after a courageous princess,
and your name means 'an offering given with both hands'.

My prayer is that you will discover the courage that God
has put inside you, and that you will always remember to
offer all things back to Him, with two open hands.

You are a treasure and a joy, and will always be my pickle.

Contents

Foreword

Most of the people I meet who share their story with me have at some point tried to figure out their destiny in life. Some haven't found it and are still carrying unfulfilled dreams in their heart; some have been so discouraged that they've stopped considering what they were made for entirely. The ones who already seem to know share their struggles on the 'long road to great'. Few I know feel like they have fully arrived – that they overcame it all and made it. I think that is because there is always a higher calling for each person, no matter what stage we are in. With God, there are always more dreams for us to dream.

The road we travel from childhood to maturity and into our adult lives is riddled with…well…'life'. So many things happen and messages are imprinted upon us, both deliberately and inadvertently, that we don't necessarily at first become the person God has intended us to be. We lay down the true desires God put in our hearts, perhaps thinking of them as childish, or feeling that we don't have the resources to accomplish them. Perhaps we think (mistakenly) we will never get a chance to fulfill these dreams. *Dare to Ask* is for anyone who has ever caught a glimpse of who they were made to be, but are still traveling that road.

When I first met Simcha we became fast friends. We share many common interests and spiritual points of view. Our families now share much time together, so I've had the pleasure of truly getting to know her. After a time, our relationship extended to also working together on many fun initiatives and most recently establishing the Ascend Carmel worship programmes.

Over the years, I've had the joy of witnessing first hand Simcha's tenacity and courage in whatever she faces in life. I've seen how she applies the truth of God's word to the situations that arise and the choices she has made along the way, both in times of weakness and in times of strength. In this book, Simcha admirably shares personal stories with great honesty and vulnerability. She then translates these personal experiences into a series of challenges for her readers to reach for more, to dare to ask God for the fullness of what He intends for their lives.

It is my firm belief that a great principle, deep within the heart of God, is that our life is not just our own. That in whatever way, great or small, our lives here on earth are about impacting others for the Kingdom of God. Simcha has a wonderful, innate desire to help people. I've watched how she naturally encourages everyone around her as an outflow of her spiritual life. She lives in such a way to purposefully support others and build them up. This book is another way that she will do that, this time for you, her reader, because this book is not just about principles, it's about real life experiences we can all connect to.

In my journey as a worship leader, I have asked myself many of the questions posed in this book. I have faced great difficulty and had to rise up in the defining moments, believing for God's greater purpose. I have also endured seasons of prolonged waiting, learning to rest in the assurance of God's goodness and kindness. Just like Simcha shares in this book, we all walk through moments of weakness and struggles, but also of joy and exhilaration in our pursuit of God. The question is, will we continually step forward with boldness and live with patience to inherit the promises of God for our lives? Will we believe what He says is true?

I am determined to see just how far God will take humble, yielded lives. It is my strong conviction that in that place, there are truly no limits with God. This book is a wonderful example of that; it will both encourage and challenge you to take hold of the opportunities presented in your daily life, and dare you to ask God for more.

Sarah Liberman
Worship Leader

Preface

Dare to Ask began as an album project. It started with a song about Rahab, called 'Dare to ask'. As I continued to write other songs, I noticed that they were following a pattern. I was writing a series of songs based on certain characteristics that were evident in some characters in the Bible. As the songs began to flow, I became fascinated by these different characters; men and women who showed tenacity and courage as they risked their lives, reputations and futures to chase after a God who, for many of them, was not even the god of their people.

The songs started evolving; no longer were they simply about particular characteristics but how I could apply their examples to my own life. I started noticing that all the songs had a common theme – daring to ask for something from the perspective of faith and trust. Of being willing to wrestle with God for more, and not to be afraid of the struggles. Always alongside of this wrestling is a rest that must be maintained. I discovered that in almost every situation I was in, there was a tension between resting in all that was, and all that God is, and yet being determined to push in for more.

Personally, I have walked through several seasons where I feel I could have been justified to see myself as a 'victim' in various scenarios. However, as these stories challenged me to change my perspective, I started noticing a transformation in my own faith and walk with God. As I allowed God to help me lay down previous patterns of thinking, and was willing to wrestle with God for the blessings I know He has for me, I was surprised to start seeing fruit in my own life. This brought with it great and surprising joy!

I decided to start writing down some of the stories of how my songs came about, firstly in the form of a blog. But somehow this blog only scratched the surface of what was stirring in my heart, and I felt I needed to write more. The result is this book. Each chapter begins and ends with a quote from the song that the chapter is based on.

While the majority of the stories contained here focus on women, this isn't intended to be a 'study' of women from the Bible, or a book only for women. It just happens that by virtue of the place that women held in society in biblical times, they best exemplify the principles I explore. However, today, these principles apply across the board to all people, in all walks of life, and the truths that are captured in these stories can be an encouragement to both men and women alike.

As I started to spend more time grappling with what God was saying to me, and digging further to understand what I had actually learned through the songs I had written, I have found myself walking through seasons and situations that echo those faced by characters we will be exploring in this book.

These times made me laugh, because they reminded me that God has a sense of humour. So often I've been heard to say, 'Don't preach what you're not prepared to go through yourself.' So here is the product of me daring to ask. My prayer is that something in this journey I've walked would resonate with your own, and that you would find encouragement to persevere.

Preface

The heart cry of this book is to encourage and challenge you to get back in touch with the inner core of who you were made to be; to dare to dream, dare to sing again....

...May you Dare to Ask.

How to use this book

At the start and end of each chapter is a quote from the song that inspired the chapter. Each chapter begins with a shorter quote, to set the scene. This can be used as a thought to meditate on, or simply to gain insight about the direction of the chapter.

At the end of each chapter a more substantial quote is given, allowing space for you to take the principles of the chapter and apply it to your own life.

Each chapter has been written in such a way that should make it applicable to you, and accessible for you at whatever stage or season you're in with your walk with God.

My prayer is that, as you read through these personal and biblical stories, you will be encouraged that God knows exactly what is going on in your life. None of it will be wasted if you're walking with Him. Even if you can't see it, understand it or perceive it know that nothing is wasted.

CHAPTER I

Dreaming with God

In Me all things are possible
In Me all things are made new
All things made perfect in My hands…
So rest your soul.

Have you ever dreamed of something, worked towards it tirelessly, imagined life as if the dream were the reality, but eventually given up on it? I think most of us have. We all have a deep place in our souls where we dream of what we could be or what could have been.

God has taken me on a journey over the past few years, of gradually restoring the things He spoke to me about through my childhood and teenage years. These included dreams that had been shot down so many times that I'd given up on them completely.

The word God gave me for the season I am currently in is; 'I am making *all* things new. I am making *old* things new'. Sometimes, in the all-inclusive use of the word 'all', we forget that this also includes the *old* things. It includes the things we left at the back of the shelf to gather dust; and it includes the things that we abandoned, shoved in a box and sealed the lid on tight. Right now, for me, God is gently taking those boxes out from the back of the cupboard, dusting them down and taking out the dreams one by one. He is revealing to me that I might be ready to handle them now.

This particular journey is so special because I know that I had closed the lid so tight on these dreams that there is no doubt that if any of them come to pass, it can only be because *He* made it happen.

Childhood dreams

Our dreams for ourselves were often God's dreams for us, before He gave them to us to dream. I haven't met many people whose dreams bear no relation to what God has made them to be – we are usually fairly self-aware in our dreaming.

I would suggest that our dreams are echoes of our call, our destiny and our purpose. Eternity is something we cannot grasp in our human nature, but yet it is where we are headed and is part of our nature:

> *He has made everything beautiful in its time.*
> *He has also set eternity in the human heart; yet*
> *no one can fathom what God has done from*
> *beginning to end. (Eccl. 3:11).*

Our souls are eternal. I believe that our dreams, those deep yearnings of our hearts, come from our soul, and should not be ignored. Often God speaks to us when we're young, in dreams, earnest desires and 'visions'. Unfortunately we can dismiss these dreams as adults, because we're so often tricked into making 'rational' and 'logical' decisions that go against the dreams we once held dear.

We can give up on our dreams because 'life gets in the way'. We think that what we're busy doing all day has nothing to do with what we spend time dreaming about in our 'down time'.

What if all the things that we think of as distractions, or even what appear as direct attacks on our dreams, are actually a part of the preparation for the fulfillment of our calling?

Some of my own childhood and adolescent dreams are still buried deep in my heart, and for the longest time I thought they were foolish, unenlightened and immature. Recently, God has challenged me in a very raw and deep way not to scoff at or disregard the things that He put in my heart.

Just because I was a child, or a young person with less life experience, doesn't mean those dreams were entirely wrong; they were simply innocent and uncorrupted.

Think of how a young child might describe or draw

something that you and they are both standing in front of. You are seeing the same thing, yet the perspective and points of reference can paint a very different picture. As a child we might be looking at the same dream, but processing it with limited understanding.

Sometimes the dreams of our childhood and youth are too big for us to handle until we are older and mature enough. And yet too often we can taint the dreams with worldly desires and ambition, rather than waiting for God's perfect hand and timing to bring them to pass.

A biblical dreamer

The perfect biblical example of this is Joseph. In Genesis 37 we see what a true dreamer he really was. Not only did he have huge dreams, but he also had absolutely no tact when describing them to his brothers! He didn't not know how to handle his dreams, or how to share them without making it sound like he was inflating his own ego – or trying to elevate himself above others.

There is no way that Joseph could have foreseen the way that his dreams would come to pass, and mostly likely he would never have chosen for life to go the route it did in order for those dreams to become a reality. He had to trust that what he had seen would come to pass, even though it seemed impossible, unlikely and probably sounded crazy to those around him.

It wouldn't surprise me if Joseph completely gave up on the dreams he had while he spent time in prison, and in captivity. How could those dreams, which had seemed to real, ever come to pass?

Of course we know from scripture that Joseph's dreams did come to pass, in ways I'm sure he could never have envisioned.

In Genesis 42 we see the fruition of the dreams that he had, with his brothers coming to Egypt and bowing down to him exactly as he had seen in his dreams. One important lesson to take from Jospeh is that the dreams God gave him, happened in God's way, and in God's time.

Restoring our dreams

Not only does God restore the dreams that He has given, but He suddenly opens our eyes to see how all the things we've walked through weave together to make us more able to fulfil our dreams. Again, this word 'all' includes those things that seemed painful or pointless. It also includes time 'wasted' in waiting. Yes, it includes *all things!*

When our dreams are realised God's way, it points to Him so much more than had we tried it our way, in our own strength.

The best thing about the journey of restoration is that we have no need to fret, worry or strive. Like a mother labouring with a child, there is definitely pushing and work to be done, but it can only come with the 'contractions', God's hand at work alongside us.

After three very different labours, believe me when I say that pushing without contractions is pointless. And when there aren't contractions, you are forced to rest.

We are not absolved of our responsibility to 'step up' when the moment requires us to act, but, at the same time, we do not have to strive to create circumstances that God has not yet ordained. If He gives us a dream but nothing seems to be happening, it is our job to rest, incubating and tending to it carefully until the time when the contractions come.

It is a constant balance we must learn, of resting in the knowledge that He will bring about all things to happen in His perfect time, but also wrestling with God for what He has said and promised. We should be in a constant state of healthy dissatisfaction, resting in all He's given but wrestling for more.

Take delight in the LORD;
And He will give you the desires of your heart.
(Psalm 37:4)

Whatever our circumstance, it is our job to delight ourselves in God, trusting that, even when it seems impossible, He can bring things about in way that defies our understanding of what is 'natural'. God created the universe so for Him all things are possible.

My story at this point in time speaks of an accumulation of seemingly impossible events, colliding into one massive blessing, which points towards many of the dreams I have carried for 30+ years. A series of completely miraculous happenings occurred, which resulted in me being put in a position where I am able to exercise so many muscles that were wasting away, and use so many gifts that were dusted over. I feel alive again!

I have still not ticked all the boxes on my dream list, but, now I am seeing that God has resurrected old dreams and brought them to life, I am able to rest in the knowledge that He can do it with any dream if it's His will. I strived and pushed my way until I got too tired, and time and time again got nowhere. The circumstances I find myself in now couldn't have been manufactured with all the striving, pushing and hard work in the world.

They are simply Him. His work. His hand. Making all things perfect.

And the best thing about this?

Rest.

My soul can breathe. He's got this. His hand is on it all. It's not hard for Him. I can breathe, exhale, find His joy in the moments and *rest*.

Do you dare to ask for His rest?

Be still and wait for me
In still and quiet I am found
I'll satisfy even the dry places
I'll take your load and set you free.

In Me all things are possible
In Me all things are made new
All things made perfect in My hands…
So rest your soul.

Be still and watch and see
Even the wind and waves will cease
I will make straight the way for you
And move mountains
I'll take your hand, and set you free.

CHAPTER 2

Dreams and destiny

All is for Your Glory,
All is for Your fame.
That on every fibre in my life would be seen
Your signature.

Dare to Ask

A few months ago, I reached a pivotal moment in my life. I had a large decision to make. An offer I received for a job was causing me to consider my calling, and how this change of pace 'fitted in' with all that I was already doing – and whether I should even be doing it at all. During this time, I listened to a sermon by John Bevere[1]. A particular quote left me shell-shocked to my core for quite some time:

> *In the end, you won't be judged by what you did,*
> *but by what you were called to do.*

How many of us give up on that which we somehow, deep down, *know* we were made to do, because life pushed us into a different box? Or we created the box we wanted God to come and fit into with us? Perhaps our dream wasn't conventional so we came to believe it couldn't be right?

When I was 17, I had had a different big decision to make: what to study at university. I was torn in two, on one hand having dreamt of pursuing a career in music from an early age, but also quite liking the thought of being a nurse or midwife.

My school encouraged me to follow the more vocational route, citing 'job security' as their main reason. I was aware that the chance of succeeding in the music world was slim to none! I asked God to make it clear to me what I was supposed to do, and that if a medical profession wasn't for me, that He would shut the door.

I was rejected from all six universities I applied to, within one week. As a student at an elite, private girls' school (where God had miraculously allowed me to study for free – a story for another day!) very few students received rejection for university places, and I had six! God had made it abundantly clear to me that I was meant to be studying music.

Letting go of entitlement

It is important to understand that timing is crucial. There are different seasons in life, and it may be that we need to be prepared to let go of the dream or the vision we have, just for a short time. I have certainly experienced this many times in my life.

I have two seemingly unrelated dreams that I've been carrying in my heart for many years: working with rescued trafficked women and children, and recording the album that inspired this book. I have no idea how either of those dreams could ever be related or work together. Maybe they're for completely different stages in my life. The question that I find myself returning to regularly is: am I prepared and at peace, in myself, for the possibility that they may never happen?

There is a tension we must learn to live with well: to be at peace that our dreams may never happen, while trusting that God placed them in our hearts for a reason. That reason may be something we don't ever come to know or understand, but we can still have peace. At the same time as finding this peace, we should commit to not letting our dreams die too soon.

My dreams and hopes for the future are not something I am entitled to, they're things God can use me through. I have to be willing to let go of them, and trust He will fulfil and facilitate them in His time. God is not obligated to make these things happen, just because I believe they should, or want them to. We must learn to live with a healthy passion of commitment to investing in our gifts, and expect God to give us situations in which our gifts can be used. But all the while it is necessary to hold onto the Maker of our dreams rather than clinging on to the dreams themselves, or making idols of them.

An open hand

Keeping an 'open hand' is a phrase often used to describe holding things lightly, which can be difficult for those things we hold close to our hearts. I was recently in a position of really having to make a choice to lay my dreams down *again*, at a point when I *could* have 'forced' them into being. But as I walked through the process of laying them down, I had to consciously decide that I wanted to do things God's way, and in God's timing. We have to be willing to *ask* God to have His way, not insist on ours being the only option.

The balance between keeping an open hand and pursuing our destiny is a difficult one to maintain. Sometimes there is a season of inward wrestling to figure out what we are supposed to be doing at this moment in time. At other times we actually have to serve someone else's vision, with the understanding that it is a season of preparation for us.

Serving someone else's vision can be a difficult task that requires patience and a commitment to serve even when you don't understand why or what you're doing! A great example of this is the relationship between Elijah and Elisha in 1 and 2 Kings. Elijah is instructed to anoint Elisha to be the prophet that will succeed him. I believe it was the purity of heart in Elisha that made Elisha the right choice for Elijah (1 Kings 19:18). He was included as one who had not bowed down and kissed the false god, Baal. This chapter ends simply with:

> *Then he set out to follow Elijah and became his servant. (1 Kings 19:21).*

We can assume that from that moment on Elisha was with Elijah in all that he did. He saw all the crazy things that happened in Elijah's role as prophet, and I would imagine at times would have felt in awe, confused, amazed and probably terrified at the things that Elijah was doing. He probably had to bite his tongue at times, and trust that God had called him to learn from this mighty prophet for a reason. He may not have even understood why, but I'm sure he trusted that Elijah knew what he was doing; after all, he had seen fire fall from heaven! (1 Kings 18).

In 2 Kings 2, it becomes evident that Elisha knew it was time for Elijah to be taken to heaven. Later we will look at the characters of Ruth and Naomi, and here we hear echoes of Ruth's words to Naomi, in how Elisha refused to leave Elijah, three times over:

> *But Elisha said, 'As surely as the Lord lives and as you live, I will not leave you.' So they went down to Bethel. (2 Kings 2:2).*

What a wonderful servant-hearted companionship. Elisha had spent time serving Elijah. We read nothing about him through all the events that happened in the previous chapters, and yet we know Elisha was with him.

Perhaps Elisha was by now so used to serving someone else's vision that the thought of stepping out into his own calling was terrifying! When Elijah insisted that *now* was the time, Elisha made his request:

> *'Let me inherit a double portion of your spirit,' Elisha replied. (2 Kings 2:9).*

In this moment he knew that the time had come for him to step out from being in a servant role, and to step into his own call. He also recognised that all the time he'd spent with Elijah had been a direct training ground for him – so much so that he asked for the same spirit as Elijah to come on himself.

When we are called to serve someone else's vision, we cannot skip the stage of serving and demand the double portion straight away. We have to put the time in and prove ourselves faithful along the way.

Sometimes we have to fully lay down what we have hopes and dreams for, accepting that the time isn't right. But during other moments we can sense we are being released into chasing our dreams with everything we have, as we watch Him open doors and bring about opportunities we never thought were possible.

Nothing is wasted

All the years I spent wondering 'why?', and 'what was that for?' were years spent hidden away with God. Though I didn't realise it at the time, I was walking through seasons of separation from the path I would have chosen for myself, in order to prepare me for what was to come. These were times when He was doing a deep work in me. He couldn't have done this any other way, as I'm far too stubborn and headstrong to recognise when God wants me to Himself!

He had to move my family to a country where we were essentially stuck, technically illegally due to disputes over our paperwork, for more than three years, to do His deep work in us. It's amazing that God can take two completely different people (my husband and I), with completely different gifts and callings, and, by moving us to this new place, released both of us into things we had only ever dreamed of.

What He is preparing you for is worth the wait. And when it's time to go, you will accomplish your destiny with so much more authority and power than you would have done if you had skipped the waiting.

A few years back, I went to a women's meeting where the topic being spoken about was the desert. I remember that she went into great detail explaining the extent of the process that a caterpillar goes through in order to transition into its new form – a butterfly.

Two things about this process really struck me and have remained as strong reminders whenever I see butterflies and caterpillars. Firstly, once a caterpillar has built its cocoon, the process it goes through inside involves it being reduced down to a soup-like consistency of about 50 cells. It is literally taken apart and its cells self-destruct. The reconstruction of this creature takes on a completely different cell structure, and transforms it into an entirely new form. The process of essentially being melted down to the bare minimum and then being recreated is a painful and seemingly gruesome one, and yet, it's something that each and every butterfly we see, goes through.

What a reflection of what we sometimes have to go through in order for God to truly bring us into the beauty of what He has for us.

The second thing that hit me about this creature is the struggle it goes through to get out of its cocoon once its transformation has been completed. Not only has it been biologically remade into a new form, it now has to struggle to get out and live!

The cocoon is made from a strong silk that the caterpillar prepares in its own body and spins around itself, which protects the caterpillar and keeps it safe and contained while undergoing the painful transforming process. However, the butterfly has to use all of its newfound strength to get out of its cocoon. What struck me most about this process is that *if the butterfly does not struggle and free itself, it will never be able to fly.*

There will be times when this truth can be applied to our own lives. Times when we have to go through the struggle, pressing on and pushing through, so that we can 'fly' as a new creation.

When my heart bleeds dry
And I'm completely undone,
I will look to You, and lift my hands.
In the morning's joy,
when my cup runs over,
I will look to You and lift my hands.

In the seasons change,
one thing remains;

All is for Your glory,
All is for Your fame.
All is for Your glory,
that on every fibre of my life
would be seen…
Your signature.

CHAPTER 3

Gifts and callings

Stay with me a while

Rest in Me and find who you truly are

You're all I want

My treasure, My love

Stay with me a while.

For my whole life I have felt called to be a musical worshipper, and to be involved in music in some way. For many years and many reasons, I wasn't given the opportunity to use my musical gift publicly, and found myself frustrated or saddened by the wait. It has taken me a while, and I have not always been successful in this, but what I have been learning is that I can always find a way to use those gifts. I'm a musician, so I can worship at home. I have worship music on, I sit at my piano, I expose my kids to lots of kinds of music and worship and I encourage them to worship. My gift isn't for me, it's been given to me to use to bless God's heart and to bless others. But that could mean me simply worshipping at home, as well as on a platform with a team.

There is a difference between a gift and a dream. Our gifts are the tools that God has put within us to equip us for the calling He has for us. We may be aware of some of these callings, in the shape of dreams that we carry in our hearts, much like Joseph did. But there may be more to our calling than the dreams we carry; they may only be the tip of the iceberg! It is our responsibility to keep our gifts sharp and usable, like a warrior, ready for action when the time comes.

I cannot think of a single gift that cannot be used to some degree at any time. For example, I have a friend, Andrew, who has the gift of teaching and preaching. He doesn't always have the platform to use this gift, but he is still determined not to let it go dormant. So he decided to find other ways to use it, and committed to posting a fresh word from God every day on a blog. He decided that he would seek what God had to say to him each day, then share it. It blesses many people to find his fresh word waiting for them in their inbox.

Sometimes Andrew writes long and meaty messages, while sometimes it's just a couple of sentences. Whatever it is, he is blessing those who are choosing to engage, and he is keeping his gifts sharp and connecting with God in the way he was best created to do. I love what he has to say about this topic:

At that which you might be gifted in – practice.

Whether music or art, leadership or giving, prayer or administration or whatever it is... build into your life a regular and public production of this gift.

Not 'public' as in 'hype-up-the-hoopla', but as in, actually do something that gets out of your head, out of your bedroom, and seeks to impact real people. Then repeat.

Learn, practice, get better, take two steps forward, be frustrated at the one back, seek advice when you get stuck, admire your heroes but don't get discouraged at the gap, and keep going.

If it's in your head, it's dead. You gotta go do.

Something has been deposited in you. Pour it out regularly for the benefit of others. Resist the natural inclination to bury it. Get better at it over time. And just keep banging away with all your might.[2]

What if your gift is hospitality but you don't have a large enough home to do what you'd like? Take your hospitality out of the house; take a batch of cakes to work or go and volunteer in a soup kitchen. Take your gift to the people you want to bless. What if your gift is to be a mother, but you don't have any kids? There are *always* people who need a mother figure in their life so ask God to point them out to you.

Stewarding your gifts well

I believe there is always a way to use your gifts. There is a difference between waiting for God's timing to release you fully into your dreams and destiny, which your gifts are there to support, and letting your gifts get blunt because God hasn't released you yet.

The Bible instructs us to steward the gifts we have. In Matthew 25:14–30, Jesus shares the parable of the talents. The men who were called 'good and faithful' servants were the ones who invested their talents, and made a gain on behalf of their master.

Jesus said that God sees what we do in the secret place (Matt. 6:6). I don't believe we should only be using our gifts when everyone around us knows about it. The servant who didn't invest his talent, so saw no return on it, let his treasure lie dormant while his master was absent. He didn't use it, he didn't invest it, he didn't share it, he didn't spend it. He just buried it, and let it sit and because of this he was called wicked!

We have all been given something, and it is our responsibility to invest it, like the first two servants. Neither of them knew what would happen when they invested their talents, nor did they know when the master was returning. Interestingly, they weren't told to invest their talents either.

They just did it, and were rewarded by their master being pleased with them.

I believe that when we invest in our dreams while in the secret place, it blesses God's heart. Resting in Him, and offering the gifts He's given us back to Him, shows us who we truly are and it shows Him that we are living as we were created to live, for an audience of One. If it is only for His eyes – it is worth it. When an audience of One is enough, we're much more likely to be given a greater audience (see Matt 25 vv.21, 23,29).

When we do the opposite, when we strive to create the circumstances to use our gifting or calling 'for all to see', we are saying to God that we care more about people's opinion of us than His. What we would view as 'successful' and fruitful ministries usually have been borne out of hours in prayer, tears in the secret place and/or worship poured out in the middle of the night.

These are the investments we should be making into our dreams and callings – in the secret place. It is God who decides if and when we are ready for release into a more prominent outworking. More often than not, I have seen this align with us being content with Him as our audience (and the possibility that He might be the only audience we will ever have).

We need also to remember that sometimes God puts gifts in us for no other purpose than to bless His heart with them. I remember one time a word given to a young man on our worship programme[3]:

> *God has put depths to your soul which you know*
> *are there, but you struggle to share with others. He*
> *put that depth there because it's just for Him. He*

*wants to have parts of you which only get shared
with Him. Your secret place and innermost depths
are a joy and a delight to Him, and you shouldn't
feel bad that you struggle to share your feelings and
thoughts with others. He made you like that on
purpose, because those parts of you are just for Him.*

Often the gift of intercession or prayer is just for Him. The role of intercessor is one who stands in the gap on behalf of others, or a situation, and presents petitions to God on their behalf. The role of an intercessor can be a lonely path, but one that is richly rewarded and *seen*. Maybe you are pouring your gift of hospitality out with your kids, and no one other than they *and He* ever see it. Is that enough? Would you be content to continue using your gifts, if no one else ever saw you doing so?

I walked through many years in which I didn't understand why I had studied what I did, because it didn't seem to set me up for anything. A lot of the passions I had in my heart actually ended up being dampened because I spent years confused about why God had so clearly guided me to study music, and given me the dream to do something for which I had no outlet.

Being aware of the war

There is a flip side to the wonderful truth that God has your destiny in hand. This is that the enemy has an understanding of your destiny also. Think about that. He knows. He was there when your destiny was written. Therefore, he is able to pinpoint the right areas to attack in his attempts to derail your destiny.

The devil understands what a mighty force a Christian fulfiling their call can have on the world, so he launches very direct attacks to try to stop them. I have started to notice a trend; some of the greatest struggles I see people walking through are, more often than not, closely connected to their gifts and calling (although they often don't connect the two). This insight has helped me gain peace and understanding, particularly in my own family.

My daughter went through a four-year struggle with selective mutism. For the majority of her life outside our home, she simply did not speak. She didn't speak in school, she didn't speak in any of her extra-curricular activities, she didn't speak to adults or children outside of our immediate family and possibly two or three of her friends. Yet she was happy. She was the happiest little thing in the world! It caused no end of concern to her teachers and other adults around us, but I didn't worry. She was completely content in life, despite the fact that she couldn't bring herself to speak in these situations. She was afraid, and we never knew why, yet we didn't feel the need to use the psychologists that were being pushed on us by her teachers and school.

In the midst of all of this, my daughter found a way to cope with her fear and figured out other ways of communicating without words. While she remained silent, she still had lots of success. She was still somehow invited to friends' houses, despite not speaking to them. Today, I believe that God spared her from a significant amount of corruption during her years of silence, because He can use all things for good.

However, there came a moment when I strongly felt that there was more to this than we were seeing on the surface. While she seemed content to remain silent, I began to sense that her voice was under attack. I also began to believe that this probably indicated that her voice was going to be a significant part of her destiny. Whether she was going to be as a singer, a worshipper, a speaker, a teacher, a doctor – whatever it may be – I realised that her voice was a threat to the enemy and he was doing his best to try and silence her. It was subtle, but the sense was very real.

So we went to war. We battled with God to help us find the right strategy to release her voice. After a significant amount of time and some remarkable miracles, He did it!

One day, I put a sofa I was trying to sell on a local website, and almost instantly got a call from an English-speaking lady (UK English, which is even more unusual!). She was interested in buying my sofa. We realised that we were both from the UK and got chatting. She was a new immigrant, and so we instantly had lots to chat about. It transpired that she was a speech therapist, specialising in selective mutism, and was looking for work. I was gobsmacked.

Here I was on the phone to the answer to prayer I had been looking for! I instantly invited her over to meet my daughter and they hit it off straight away. My daughter's road to recovery and 'normalcy' started, and our first miracle had been witnessed.

After several months of hard work, our precious girl is now released to speak at school and converses happily with adults. She talks in many situations that she was never able to before, all with an inner peace and confidence that bear the hallmarks of God's work in her through those years of silence.

I have seen many examples of this form of direct attack, focused on the area that God created us for. Sometimes, however, the enemy launches a much more subtle attack.

This comes in the form of a general wearing down, weariness or lethargy and a dullness through all the hassles that 'life' throws at us.

The result?

We no longer function within our calling, or use our gifts.

We need to be aware of this facet of spirituality. While we are able to learn some of the enemy's tactics through the Bible, we often don't give him enough credit. He is an expert deceiver, intent on discouraging and derailing us from pursuing our dreams.

Standing firm

It is important to remember that while we are not *saved* by our works, we *will* be held to account for what we do with our lives, and how we steward the dreams and gifts that He has given us (as we saw in the parable of the talents). I believe many of us need reawakening to the intentions God had for us when He first put those dreams in our hearts. He equips us for what we're made to do, giving us the skills, as well as the equipment we need to fight the enemy. If we'd only use it!

> *Finally, be strong in the Lord and in his mighty power. Put on the full armour of God, so that you can take your stand against the devil's schemes.*
> *(Eph. 6:10)*

I pour myself before you My King
I've nothing to bring but myself
Nothing of worth
No worldly treasure.
Just me with You
At Your feet
And you say:

Stay with Me a while

Rest in Me and find who you truly are

You're all I want

My treasure, My love

Stay with me a while.

CHAPTER 4

Dare to ask

Can I come with you?
Do I dare to ask?
Can I join with you?
Do I let this moment pass?

One of my favourite Bible stories is that of Rahab.

I have always been struck by how bold Rahab was to ask the Hebrew spies to let her and her family join their people. Rahab was a prostitute and a gentile, so it is fairly safe to say that she would have been classified as 'unclean', and, of course…she was a woman.

We know very little about Rahab; she first appears in Joshua 2, when the king of Jericho hears there are spies in the land so communicates with her to ask about their whereabouts. It makes me wonder: how had she grabbed the attention of the king? Was this a regular occurrence? Was she a trusted confidante, perhaps even a 'spy' for the king? How had the spies found her? Did the king's guards see them enter her house?

She may well have been someone the king depended on for news from the outside world, such as information on who was coming in and out of the city walls. Her situation and occupation would have meant she was well placed to gather such information.

Due to her position at the city walls (or, more likely, *in* the city walls), she would have known of the Israelites. The Bible says that she informed the spies that there was fear in the land, and that 'all who live in this country are melting in fear because of you' (Josh. 2:9).

Rahab had clearly heard about the Israelites and the wonders their mighty God performed. Maybe she had picked this up from other men she had entertained, from the elders at the gates or from the market place – or possibly from all these sources.

Rahab was not the only person in Jericho who had heard that the Israelites were coming, but she *was* the only one who took action. Her actions suggest that she wasn't satisfied with her status quo. Rabbinical teachings[4] suggests that Rahab was most likely well known and prosperous. She probably had a luxurious, 'easy' life, but all the while I believe that she would have been acutely aware of how she was acquiring it, and maybe even subconsciously, longed for a way out.

A stirring inside

When I read Rahab's story, I see hints of an internal desperation to leave her life behind, as if she was yearning for something more. Perhaps she had been dreaming for many years about a better life, and somehow she knew this was her chance to grasp hold of it.

Perhaps she had a suspicion that this foreign God was not pleased with what was going on inside the city walls. Whatever her suspicions, Rahab knew that destruction was looming for her city, and yet something inside of her wanted life, and she was determined to grasp hold of life where she had discerned it.

The name Rahab has a few meanings, one of which is 'fierceness'[5], and in Joshua 2:4 the first indication of this characteristic appears. She hid the spies, and dared to lie to the king's men who were looking for them. Not only this, but she proceeded to send them on a wild goose chase into the hills for three days! Her actions would certainly have warranted a death sentence for treason if the king had found out. Rahab was not just desperate for a change; she was also tough enough to take a huge risk to ensure she got it.

Rahab may have rebelled against the king's men, but she deeply respected the God of the Israelites. Stories and rumours had been spreading around the city: stories about miracles, clouds of glory and pillars of fire; stories about an awesome and mighty God who lived *among* His people, personally leading them and providing for them supernaturally.

Rahab had heard these stories and she wanted in. She wanted to be a part of this story; she wanted to belong to this God.

When the spies arrived in the city, she saw it as her moment. I love how Rahab *threw* herself at it with complete abandon; she was prepared to die for it; she had such courage, such tenacity, such chutzpah[6]!

After hiding the spies, and with them in her debt, Rahab acknowledged that their God is the One, true God, and took the opportunity to make her bold request (Josh. 2:12–13). She dared to ask for a complete change in circumstance for all of her family, knowing that if they were spared as the spies had promised, they would be able to join the Israelites. Perhaps, more importantly, they would be able to come under the wing of the incredible God.

Waiting well

So, Rahab made her request, and then she waited.

Waiting is important. Waiting is never a waste of time. Waiting is what gets us ready for what's coming.

As instructed by the spies, Rahab gathered her family into her home and kept a red cord hanging in the window, which was the sign that would show the Israelites where she was and that she was ready to be rescued.

As the Israelites circled Jericho for the seventh time on the seventh day, Joshua instructed them to 'Shout! For the LORD has given us the city' (Josh. 6:16), adding the instruction to keep Rahab and her family safe.

Can you imagine the reaction of the people when they were told that they had to spare a prostitute and her family? They must have thought that Joshua had gone astray, or perhaps gone mad!

The Bible is clear on what Joshua's instructions were regarding the saving of Rahab (Josh. 6:17), but I can imagine the murmurs and thoughts of the people in reaction to such a command going something like this:

> *There is a prostitute who needs to come with us?…I mean…The spies we sent in the land stayed with her? I thought they were trusted warriors, men of God and purity? There has to be more to this story than this? What's going on?*

Red: the colour of redemption

There are a few things that I love about Rahab's story. Firstly, we've seen just how gutsy she was. She had a plan and threw herself at it with everything she had. She wasn't prepared to let the opportunity for change to pass her by. She risked everything for a new chapter.

But, perhaps more than this, I love the redemptive meaning carried through the scarlet chord.

Red chords could very well have indicated the trade of prostitution. What were red chords back then, became the red lights we know of today. So the chord was the very thing that defined who Rahab was. A red chord hanging in the window could have signalled to travellers where they could find company for the night.

Once the Israelites heard about Rahab and saw the red chord in the window, they would have known who she was and what she did for a living, as there was no hiding it. The people walked passed her window every day for seven days, and then seven times on that final day. Some of the Israelites may have been praying for the salvation of that poor 'sinner's' soul!

But for Rahab, the value of what she hoped would come far outweighed the shame of what had passed. For her the chord symbolised hope.

The word for 'chords' in Hebrew comes from the root '*Tiqvah*', which means hope. With hope comes expectation and anticipation. Rahab was being asked 'hang her hope' in the window for the sake of her salvation!

It seems that Rahab would have rather paraded her past in front of thousands as they passed her window, than risk not having a future. Sometimes we have to be willing to humble ourselves in order for our inheritance to be realised...

Being humbled

While on a leadership training course several years ago, a leader asked to meet with me as they felt there were some things to discuss. I happily went to this meeting not realising that this was about to be one of the most humiliating and discouraging events of my life.

I was asked to step down and to stop participating in the course, because they 'didn't really see any potential in me', and I 'didn't possess the leadership skills they were looking for'.

I was absolutely devastated. I quietly quit the course, blaming it on circumstances surrounding me, and essentially crawled under a metaphorical rock and believed every word that had been spoken over me. I was utterly humiliated. I had been working hard coordinating a large, countywide team, and many youth, pouring myself out in mentoring them, discipling them, writing courses for teens as well as serving in our local congregation. Someone had seen this, and yet deemed it all 'not good enough'.

Now, there may well have been some truth in the words that were spoken. It might have been that I was not fully ready for certain aspects of leadership at that particular moment, and it may well even have been right for me to step down from the course. But the words were spoken decisively and felt like a judgement of me as a whole, rather than specific points for improvement that I could work on.

I felt like I'd failed an exam, only this time my life had been the test, and I hadn't been aware that I was being examined.

It took me a long time to realise that while these words may have been spoken with good intention, they ended up being used as a direct attack on what God actually had in store for me. However, looking back, I see that the period of time while I was living under my rock was a very formative time. I was being moulded by being at home with a new baby which arrived shortly after. I was learning how to serve in the smallest and most mundane of ways, I was being prepared.

I did not have to parade my past before millions as they walked past my window, but I did feel as though people had been watching, judging and coming to their own conclusions about my abilities and gifts without my ever being aware of it.

The humility of stepping aside, having your confidence smashed and being 'hidden' for a season is hard, and often depressing, but never a waste of time *if* we allow God to use it. It's a choice not to fester and hold on to offense, and to trust that God had a reason and good purpose for what happened to us.

Of course, it's easy to write all this in hindsight, but I do remember that season where I was deeply hurt. I eventually did have to make a choice to not let it define me, and to forgive the leader for their lack of empathy for my feelings. I also had to trust that there was purpose for me being removed from the programme I was on.

In this case, I believe that I had to stop thinking of myself as an 'up and coming' leader, primarily because God was about to move us on from that place, but also because He knew that I needed to spend some years serving others. This had to be done from a place of humility.

As we saw in the story of Elisha, serving someone faithfully involves putting your own desires on the altar and pushing theirs forwards, even when you disagree! I believe that now, as I have been placed in different roles that involve both leadership and serving others, God is allowing me to see that those words all those years ago were not entirely correct, yet He did want me to learn learn something. He wanted me to become a certain kind of leader, which my season 'in hiding' started to prepare me for.

My inheritance from this time stem from the lessons learned and situations used for good and for His glory. Those words that were first taken to be destructive are now producing life.

Redemption and royalty

In Rahab's story, it was the same red chord that revealed her shame that brought about her deliverance. The very sign that condemned her as an unclean woman, as someone who was 'beyond saving', was what God used to redeem her and her family. The chord represented the way to life; it was redeemed as a sign of freedom.

Rahab's story did not end with her rescue. She became a free woman and an honoured woman, marrying a mighty Israelite man, Salmon, who happened to be one of the spies she had hidden. Together, they had a baby – Boaz. Boaz married Ruth. Ruth and Boaz had a baby – Obed. Obed was father to Jesse, Jesse the father to David – and David, Israel's great king, as we know, carried the line to the eternal King, Jesus. Yes, Rahab's story is one of amazing redemption!

Willing to risk it all

In the same way that Rahab grabbed a moment that came her way, and did not let it go, so can we. She was tenacious and courageous, and fought for a change in her circumstances in a way that you don't often see. She refused to accept that the events occurring around her were coincidence, she believed there was a reason something was happening, and, even though she hadn't had an encounter with the God of Israel herself, she knew He was behind it all.

I believe that as believers in 'Christianised' contexts, we have lost some of our ability to fight tenaciously for higher ground. He is always calling us higher, closer to Him, to take steps forward, to take new risks, to adventure with Him. However, our comfortable life makes it so hard to hear Him, so hard to see the path ahead and so very difficult to feel the need for more. It is not about grabbing moments to self promote or elevate ourselves, rather to keep our spiritual eyes open to see opportunities that God could be bringing our way, and be willing to take them.

In the moment Rahab decided to help the spies, she had her eyes opened to see the opportunity for change. She was able to find her freedom and joined the lineage of the Messiah, along with several other surprising women, chosen by God to prepare the way for Him. What is happening in our lives today can also indicate moments for change. We may not have foreign spies knocking on our door (although that could be pretty exciting!), but our Maker is beckoning to us to grab each moment and see where He leads us. We just have to open our eyes, listen and be willing to take a risk.

We have to dare to ask…

I heard the rumours,
Of rivers running dry,
Of seas parted, and clouds of Glory.

I heard the rumours
Of nature at their command,
A God that goes before them,
And follows up behind.

Can I come with you?
Do I dare to ask?
Can I join with you?
Do I let this moment pass?

The crimson ties
Do not hold me now.
What held me slave
Now brings freedom.
No longer defining
The hidden parts of me.
Redeemed for good
Crimson set me free.

I found my freedom
In a bargain I dared to make,
In a God who welcomed me
And even came for me

CHAPTER 5

Grabbing your kairos moment

Pick me up,

Make me an altar,

Bringing pleasing sacrifice to You.

Even with your water flowing through me,

Your fire can fall,

So wash over me, again and again.

$\mathcal{W}$e weren't accidentally born for this time. We didn't 'just so happen' to stumble into this point in history out of the blue. God didn't haphazardly bring us into the world for now...

He planned it all.

Imagine the most complicated, detailed wedding plan in the history of wedding plans. Every single detail needs to be tailored to the particular attendees. Who needs to be near who, which aunt has to be on the opposite side of the room to which uncle. Which friend would like to meet a nice man? The list goes on... It's very complicated, even for only 50 guests.

Now imagine that all of humanity is coming to this wedding feast, and all of time is leading up to it. God has planned out the whole 'seating plan', down to every last detail. Who will cross paths with who and what event specific people need to be around for.

He's got it all under control.

This is how humanity is organised: it's not coincidental, haphazard or chaotic. It's ordered, planned and strategic. It has a purpose.

Kairos (καιρός) is one of the ancient Greek words for time. It means the right or opportune moment or, the supreme moment. A kairos moment can therefore be defined as 'a moment for action or decision'. It is a moment when the future could go in drastically different directions. We saw in the last chapter that Rahab had her kairos moment when she took the courage to make her outrageous request. She recognised that moment as being the one that could take her future in a completely different direction – and she grabbed it.

Have you ever had moments like that?

The difference between a significant moment, one that might 'wow' us, and a kairos moment, lies in the call to action. It's one thing to recognise a significant moment, but it is not a moment of change if it does not lead us to action. When faced with a kairos moment, it is not enough to just be moved deeply; we are required to make bold steps.

As we've seen, for Rahab, it involved making a courageous deal with foreign people and risking her life to do so. For others, the 'action' might be to stay put, having been ready to leave.

These moments of action often go against our natural instincts. They may oppose the culture around us, whether in our families, congregations or communities. But if it isn't a moment that causes us to wake up and reassess the situation for what it is, then it isn't a kairos moment.

These moments appear in so many places in Scripture, so let's look at a few now.

Tamar: standing up for her rights

Tamar was a woman who had to fight for her rights. You can read her story in Genesis 38. In her culture and at this point in history, security and inheritance were provided through children. As a childless widow of Judah's eldest son, Er, who God struck down, the responsibility to provide her family an heir was the responsibility of Er's two brothers.

The second brother in the family, Onan, denied her this right, taking advantage of her in the process. He did not wish to further his dead brothers line, but didn't mind 'using' Tamar along the way, giving the appearance the he was doing his duty. So God also took his life. At this point, she had to wait for the third brother, Shelah, to reach adulthood. When he did so, he was not given to her in marriage, as Judah was sure he would die also. Tamar was, at this point, considered a cursed woman, appearing to have caused two men's deaths, with a father-in-law who, who refused to give her her right to offspring because of it. Forced to take extreme measures, she was determined to ensure she got her rightful inheritance.

Tamar's kairos moment came when she decided to risk it all and trick her father-in-law in order secure her rights to a child. Tamar's actions don't compute with us today; they are foreign and seem extreme, unnecessary and morally questionable. And yet we need to remember that Tamar lived in an age when duty and family honour was the backbone of society.

Tamar would have been honouring her father's wishes by marrying Er in the first place. Their marriage would most likely have occurred in order to create an alliance, or elevate status between families. It is highly unlikely that Tamar would have married for love. And, once married, she would have had two fathers to honour.

She had a sense of duty to her own father to honour his decision in his choice of husband for her, and to her father-in-law to multiply his family line. Added into this would have been her acute awareness that if she could not produce sons she would be alone, viewed as cursed and likely abandoned in her old age.

When Tamar decided to trick Judah into sleeping with her (see Gen. 38:13–19) she ran with the risk that he could have recognised her and faced the shame that would come to both of them. Yet, though we cannot fathom this behaviour in today's society, at this point in history, it was a matter of honour; she had to step out for the sake of her inheritance. As a result, she became pregnant with Judah's son. She was no longer a childless widow but became a woman of honour, esteemed by Judah and in the lineage of the Messiah. Judah himself respected her for her determination to bring honour to himself and his family, saying 'She is more righteous than I, since I did not give her to my son Shelah' (Gen. 38:26).

Possibly the most beautiful thing about the story between Tamar and Judah is the inadvertent redemption that Tamar brought to Judah.

Judah was a son of rejection. In Genesis 29 we read how Jacob, his father, had been tricked into the marriage with Leah, Judah's mother, who wasn't loved by Jacob (Gen. 29:31–35). This seed of rejection would have carried heavily in Judah's heart, and perhaps this is what caused his sons to end up with the fate they received.

Tamar fought to do things the 'right' way, to ensure the family had a continuing line. As a result, she provided Judah with offspring named Perez, which means 'breakthrough', and Zerah, meaning 'scarlet' or 'brightness'.

For me, I read a wonderful sense of peace in the response of Judah. He simply honoured Tamar, the woman who brought about multiplication in his line when he had set her aside. He didn't have muster up any grand words, or make a big show of emotion. It's like he had a sudden realisation of what she had done and why! The woman who brought about acceptance of him, when he had denied her. The woman who had brought his breakthrough when he had given up hope…

We all have people around us who have given up hope. Maybe that person is us! I think almost everyone can identify how it feels to seem cast aside, passed over, ignored or even outright denied. I certainly can. I remember reaching a point where the number of times I'd been passed over was so many, that I started believing I deserved it, and that I had nothing to offer.

All it took to break this cycle was one person. One person to consistently believe in me, gently push me, encourage me and rebuild me (probably without even realising they were doing so). This person brought hope where I had given up hope, and saw me when no one else saw me. It was this person who taught me to believe in the gifts and inheritance that God had for me again, much as Tamar did for Judah.

We should never underestimate the gift and breakthrough that we can give to others around us through an act as simple as believing in them.

Ruth: choosing a new home

What about Ruth? She was a Moabite, from a nation that was an enemy of Israel. The two nations had been at war with each other for generations. The Moabite people were actually the fruit of the incest between Lot and his daughters (Gen 19:30–38). Not only that, but Eli-Melech, Naomi's husband, Ruth's father-in-law, had left Israel, the land of his inheritance, and travelled to Moab during a time of famine (see Ruth 1:1). He had therefore taken his sons away from their promised land and moved them into a foreign land with foreign gods.

Needless to say, it did not go well for the family. Imagine the weariness that Naomi would have felt moving to a foreign land where she could never fully fit in. Then add to this the grief of losing a husband and the pain and heartbreak of outliving all of her children! Within the first few verses of the book of Ruth, Naomi had no one left apart from her two Moabite daughters-in-law. All that remained was her identity as an Israelite in a foreign land, and a longing to return to her homeland.

Both Ruth and Naomi had amazing pivotal moments in their stories. They happened at the same time, yet for entirely different reasons. Naomi's moment came in her decision to *leave* Moab, and Ruth's moment came in her decision to *stay* with Naomi.

It would have made far more sense for Ruth to have gone home and remarry, as Orpah had decided to (see Ruth 1:14). There was no certainty or promise of a future with Naomi.

Yet, like Rahab, Ruth decided to attach herself to the God of Israel. She gave up everything else, and was caught up in a wonderful story of redemption, romance and, ultimately, salvation.

The few lines of text we read do not do justice to the enormity of Ruth's decision. The Moabites were not accepted in the presence of Israel. So Ruth must have realised that she would most likely be rejected and never fit in. There was no Google for her to use to practise the language, learn the customs or check the weather at that time of year.

When Ruth made her decision, she took a bold step of faith into a completely unknown situation.

Ruth's speech to Naomi has since become famous. It is even more incredible when you understand that these women's people were at war with one another:

> *But Ruth replied, 'Don't urge me to leave you or to turn back from you. Where you go, I will go, and where you stay I will stay. Your people will be my people and your God my God. Where you die, I will die, and there I will be buried. May the Lord deal with me, be it ever so severely, if even death separates you and me.' (Ruth 1:16–17).*

Here were two broken women: widowed, people-less and childless. They were the epitome of outcasts. Yet they were determined to go home.

This moment not only changed Ruth and Naomi's futures, but all of history with it. It brought yet another 'outsider' and placed her in the centre of the greatest story of all time, the honoured lineage of the Messiah.

Esther: for such a time

In the book of Esther, we see that Esther had a very particular destiny, but she did not see her kairos moment immediately. Like Moses many years before her (Exod. 4:10,12), she did not recognise her own influence with the king. She did not feel able to take the risk. In chapter four of the book of Esther, Mordecai sends word to Esther, asking her to plead with the king on behalf of her people.

Esther's initial response is clear. She had come to accept palace life as the status quo and the unspoken message behind her message to Mordecai may well have been[7]:

> *You just don't get it. There's absolutely no way you understand life in the palace, because, if you did, there's no way you'd have asked such a ridiculous request of me. It's not just impossible – my life is at stake here!*

In the natural, Esther was right. Approaching the king uninvited was a risky idea. But Mordecai was not worried by her response, and his own has been made famous across the generations:

> *For if you remain silent at this time, relief and deliverance for the Jews will arise from another place, but you and your father's family will perish. And who knows but that you have come to your royal position for such a time as this? (Esth. 4:14).*

His words hit home.

Esther decreed a three-day fast, after which she would go to the king, accepting: 'And if I perish, I perish' (Esth. 4:16).

Acting on a kairos moment often necessitates taking a risk and, with it, facing fear. Altering the course of your life by acting on a moment that God has ordained is always going to be contested. The last thing the enemy wants is a generation of people to understand their calling and walk in their gifts. He will do everything in his power to derail our destinies and bring doubt and confusion into our minds.

Grabbing our moments

One of my own kairos moments, in which I faced both risk and fear head on, came when I was on a visit to India. My husband and I had begun to hear from God that He was calling us abroad. One of my greatest passions has always been to work with victims of trafficking, particularly young women and children in the rehabilitation process. An opportunity to go to Mumbai and teach at a Bible college came up for us, so we thought we'd use the opportunity to go and check it out as a potential place to move to.

We knew this move would entail great risk to our own children (I was pregnant at the time), as Mumbai is not a safe city for children to be raised – especially when our children were to be paler skinned, and I would be working directly with children rescued from brothels. I was perfectly aware that I would probably spend most of my time in fear that they would be snatched and sent to work in the brothels themselves. It was a very real risk.

Despite all the reservations and very real concerns we had about this move, we had a great time even with me wrestling with morning sickness. While there, I went to visit some rescue homes, spending time with victims. I was even asked to run a workshop for some children who had been recently rescued from brothels, the youngest of whom were only four or five years old. The offer was clearly extended to me to go back and work with these beautiful girls again, and I felt like my heart, while being smashed to smithereens, had found its home. So strong was this feeling that we both knew we had to go home and prepare our lives to move to Mumbai.

The next season of our life was spent 'closing down shop', finishing our training, leaving our jobs and cutting our ties, while doing research into all the aspects of moving to another country, and making sure we were ready to leave. It was then that a second moment came, almost two years later, in a meeting that neither of us can remember the details of now.

The only memory that remains is that after this meeting we both knew, without a shadow of a doubt, despite all of the planning and preparation for a life in India, that we had to move to Israel instead. India would play its part in our lives one day, but it was not for now.

It was a total kairos moment, one of our most memorable, and one that took our lives in a drastically different direction through God's graceful leading and guidance. Notice that there were two moments for us. One happened in India when we were stirred to make preparations to move. We acted on this 'wake up' moment, returning to finish our commitments and deal with our affairs. The second 'wake up' moment took all that preparation and put it in the right place.

Sometimes we don't recognise the events around us as opportunities for potential change. We often need reoccurring prompts. Thank God that He has the patience to keep prodding us. He does not give up on us.

God's timing

There was more than one kairos moment in Esther's life, too. She had every excuse to be distracted along the way, the journey from humble, orphan Jew to queen of the land is just one example!

Her story has so many 'lucky breaks' or 'coincidences', but not one detail in it was accidental. God absolutely planned for each person to be born to the right family at the right time, in the right political situation and at the right location. God's name is stamped all over her story, even though He is not mentioned by name even once in the entire book of Esther.

What about Moses? At a time when all baby boys his age were being brutally murdered (Exod. 11:5), he was somehow hidden for three months without being found. How?

Was it Moses' location? Maybe. Was he an extraordinary baby who didn't cry? Maybe? Did he have a more amazing mother than any other baby? Probably!

Whatever the reason, it was planned that way. The destiny over *this* particular baby's life was being preserved in an inexplicable way, when other lives around him were being so brutally disposed of.

> *'As the heavens are higher than the earth, so are my ways higher than your ways and my thoughts than your thoughts'* **(Isa. 55:9)**.

What do all these stories, and many others in Scripture have in common?

Time.

At some point in each story, the protagonist was in a position to perfect the art of listening.

They were sitting.

Waiting.

Rahab had no guarantee that the spies would keep their word – she had to wait and trust while the walls around her literally came crashing down.

Tamar had to wait from the death of her husband, Er, through Onan's continual humiliation, until Shelah reached the age of marriage. Then, when Shelah wasn't given to her and she took matters into her own hands, she had to wait until her pregnancy was confirmed. And the waiting continued for a little longer still, until the end of her term. She had to wait to confirm she had a son and heir, as there were no pregnancy tests or ultrasounds to give an answer sooner.

Esther's wait came from the moment she decided to go before the king, and then again from the moment the words left her lips until his reply.

And there are so many more examples in Scripture...

David had time – from his anointing through to becoming king.

Bathsheba had time. From the act of adultery, through her pregnancy to the birth of Solomon, including all the time of mourning for her firstborn who died (not to mention her husband who David had murdered). She also had to wait from Solomon's birth to the moment he was chosen as king, while King David's family was torn apart from the inside. (You can read her story in 2 Samuel 11 through to 1 Kings 1).

Time is a sacrifice.

It is easy to think that if we sit and do nothing then it's a waste of time. But was it a waste of time for Moses to live with the Midianites before he went back to Egypt? Or for Esther to undergo beauty treatments for a whole year as she prepared to go before the king for the first time? Or for Rahab to wait for the Israelites to return?

These examples were important seasons of waiting, which prepared the individuals for the next step in their destiny. Your kairos moment could be upon you right now – or right around the corner. It may require real tenacity; the boldness to dare to ask God for what's next, like Jacob did in Genesis 32: 22–32. He was bold enough to *not let go* of God while he demanded His blessing.

Positioning ourselves well

We are often given moments where we can choose to battle for more, like Jacob did, or we can continue with life as it is, not even noticing the moment that has just passed us by.

Esther could have bypassed the three days of prayer and fasting and gone immediately before the king. Instead she chose to press in and seek a miracle, through the humility of fasting and corporate prayer. She chose to step out into a battlefield – and prepared well in order to do so.

My brother has a story that involves less threat of death, but challenged me on a deep level nonetheless. He and his wife recognised that they had got very comfortable in their lives. They had good jobs, a nice house, lovely friends, a new car and bit of spare cash at the end of each month.

The potential to fall into complacency worried them, so they decided to plan to move in order to seek God for how they could get out of their comfort zone. They desperately didn't want to end up becoming 'blunt tools' in God's hands.

As it happened, God caused every plan that they made to fall through, each time making it clearer that they were meant to stay put. They did not end up moving, but a lot of their circumstances changed along the way, bringing renewed purpose and insight into why they needed to stay. During this time, the various challenges that arose made them much more dependent on God.

I really admire the heart behind their actions. They had a determination to stay sharp and to chase after God's highest. They were not giving any place over to complacency and all that comes with it; apathy, dulled spiritual gifts and blurred vision.

Esther did the same thing; she made the decision to call her people to prayer. The recognition of the necessity of prayer was a powerful moment. She accepted the challenge, and understood the reason why *she* had been placed in her position for that particular time.

I love how Robert Sterns describes some of the biblical characters: 'We serve the God of Moses the stutterer, David the adulterer, Joseph the dreamer, Elijah the scared, Gideon the youngest and Esther the orphan.'[8]

So often we can spend time admiring the amazing heroes of our faith in their 'finished' or end, heroic state, that we forget that along the way they were just ordinary men and women. They were humans like us; what set them apart was that they purposefully positioned themselves with the God of Israel and dared to ask for something more.

I rest, in Your river,
a small stone of no consequence.
I rest, in Your river,
washed clean by You.

Pick me up,
make me an altar.
Bringing pleasing sacrifice to You.
Even with water flowing through me,
Your fire can fall.

Flow through me,
living waters flow
sweep away the counterfeit.

Let truth overflow,
like joy everlasting,
let living waters flow,
and fuel the fire

I rest, at your altar,
a small stone of no consequence.
I rest, at your altar,
consumed by refining fire

These stones shall be,
a lasting memory,
a living legacy of Your story.

CHAPTER 6

Inverted kairos moments

Who am I
That You would use me?
Who am I
That You would speak through me?
I'm just a broken vessel,
Made whole by You.

We have already looked at kairos moments that happen in our own lives, I'd now like to turn this idea on its head.

In this day and age, it's so easy for life to become very individualistic. Our generation has become transfixed with itself. Our focus is on our *own* comfort, our *own* well-being, our *own* success, without a thought spared to those around us.

While on a trip, I was challenged by my dear friend and colleague, Sarah Liberman, who was speaking to a group on the Ascend Carmel worship programme, in the ancient city of Caesarea. She was speaking about the vomitarium. This is an area in the Ancient Roman amphitheatre that was specifically designated as a place where one could vomit to create more space for more feasting. For me, this sums up the culture of Ancient Rome. It was the epitome of gluttony, self-glorification and excess. Sadly today's western society can be described in much the same way.

The funny thing about physical gluttony, however, is that the feeling that usually prompts us to stop eating or to share our food actually disappears the more we eat. This means that we're tricked into believing we have space for more, or even *need* more food than our bodies can handle. This happens when we indulge our bodies with too much food, but I believe it happens spiritually too. We can feed and feed and feed, with little giving or sharing.

I'm not describing the healthy dissatisfaction and the desperation for more of God. What I'm talking about is going from meeting to meeting, worship course to seminary, from teacher to leader, getting counselling for this and ministry for that. This is when we get more and more fed, but never grow up spiritually. Paul describes this perpetual infancy: 'I gave you milk, not solid food, for you were not yet ready for it.

Indeed, you are still not ready. (1 Cor. 3:2).

In this state of infancy, we also don't ever see anything flow out from within us into the surrounding world. With no real view to the outside world, if we are not careful, we can get stuck in a place where we are no longer a vessel that God can use easily or freely. We can become those with spiritual stomachs that have tricked us into thinking we need more 'food' before we will be satisfied and can make an impact. Sometimes we can even begin to believe that we don't need to make an impact at all.

I would suggest that dreaming with God should naturally come with an element of outward focus, that God's blessings for us almost always bless others in the process.

There are some dreams that we have in our hearts that may seem less 'spiritual' and even perhaps 'selfish', and yet hidden within them is a secret to the way that God has designed us to bless and impact those around us.

Take the following example, a real dream of more than one person I know: 'I dream of living in a huge ranch, with horses roaming freely around me'.

It would be so easy for me to dismiss this as 'selfish' or 'self-centred'. I could respond to them by saying, 'How dare you, as a believer, live in a large home while thousands live in poverty?' This might seem like a valid question, but scratch beneath the surface of a desire like this and there might the essence of who that person has been created to be. Perhaps they are someone with the gift of hospitality who wishes to have an open house to welcome people into, and offer rest and retreats to those in need. Or maybe God is calling them to foster and adopt children from broken homes or war-torn countries.

All of a sudden, a seemingly 'unspiritual' dream can make more sense. I know many people who dream of larger homes to be able to serve God as they believe they are called to, through the gift of hospitality. It's always good to ask God to help us dig deeper beneath the surface of dreams we have (or others share with us), to see what the natural, 'human' dreams say about our God-given destinies.

Once we have unravelled some of the reasons why we have those dreams, it can help us steward what we have been given. Maybe having a large house isn't going to happen soon, or even at all, but how can I use my gift of hospitality *today*? It is only when we are faithful in the small things that God begins to give us more (as we saw with the parable of the talents).

Rahab certainly had one of those dreams that left a legacy. She desired to join the Israelites, and somehow become a part of them; she wanted to be truly at one with them, not just an outside observer. Rahab did receive the desires of her heart, and not only did she save her whole family, but she was grafted into the story of the Messiah Himself. She certainly couldn't have foreseen what an impact her joining the Israelites would have to endless generations after her!

Dreaming and hearing for others

I believe that we can see God and truly witness His work when we dream with Him for the sake of others.

Jesus taught that we should 'love your neighbour as yourself' (Mark 12:31), and said, 'Greater love has no one than this: to lay down one's life for one's friends' (John 15:13). These verses apply to every area of our lives, including how we dream. Our dreams are as much for others as for ourselves, if not more so.

Sarah Liberman often challenges the young people we meet in ministry with the concept of legacy. It is a common misconception that we should only start thinking about the legacy we will leave as we enter the latter stages of life, whereas we can actually start working on it much earlier. In the same way that we should be ready to receive and be 'called up' by those around us, we too can always seek God for how those around us can be encouraged, blessed and impacted.

Proverbs 18:21 says that, *'The tongue has the power of life and death'*. What an awesome privilege (and responsibility) it is when we speak to others. I have heard countless testimonies of how God has used even the most fleeting comment from one person to entirely change the life of another. How much more will that happen, then, if we are actively seeking opportunities to bless and encourage?

A couple I know are two of the most phenomenal people I've ever met. Whenever we spend time together we laugh, we tell stories, we play games, we pray, we worship. Whatever it is that we do, I *always* leave challenged, I'm *always* encouraged as a parent, as a believer and as a worshipper.

I am blessed to be surrounded by those who have this effect on me. Another example is an entire family; the kids rival their parents in their ability to spur others on! The parents often step aside, unselfishly letting their children 'take the spotlight' in times of ministry. The result is that these three kids constantly amaze me by the depth of their walk with God at such a young age, by the authenticity of their worship and their ability to work together as a team. We should never be afraid to be challenged by people younger than ourselves.

My point here is that age is insignificant. I have been challenged by my daughter's best friend, who is eight years old – perhaps in a different way, but no less powerfully than I have been challenged by a mature leader who has been 50 years in the ministry.

We should always be ready to learn from others of any age, in the same way we hope others would be willing to learn from us. When we dream with God and chase Him with all that we are, we're never too young to leave a legacy.

I would like to suggest that when we flip the idea of the kairos moment on its head, and start asking God to enable us to bring such moments to *other* people's lives, we may feel more 'filled up' spiritually than ever before.

The concept of the inverted kairos moment is simple. When we open our eyes and ears to see and hear the needs of others, God can use us to bring about moments in the lives of others. It may be the smallest moment of encouragement or something that entirely changes in the trajectory of their lives.

What would it look like if an entire generation stopped focusing inwardly and started asking to hear the heartbeat of God for others?

What would it look like if we took a moment to filter our wonderful dreams for ourselves, and started asking God who these dreams are *actually* meant to bless?

What would it look like if we started asking God to show us a glimpse of how *He* sees those around us?

What if we started thinking more about leaving a legacy of encouragement and growth in our steps, rather than feeding ourselves up?

Through His eyes

A couple of months ago my husband shared something that changed my understanding of the Great Commission completely. I learned that the word 'go' (Matt. 28:19–20) does not capture all that is contained within the text.

The Greek word that we get 'go' from, is 'πορευθέντες'. It's not a command, but a continuous action, meaning 'while you are walking'. This is interesting in and of itself, but there is also the additional fact that even though the New Testament writers were writing in Greek, they were still living in a Hebraic culture. This means the phrase takes on new levels of meaning.

In the Hebrew Scriptures, the word 'walk' means far more than just a physical action. For example, Enoch 'walked' with God (Gen. 5:35). Noah 'walked' with God, and this 'walking' refers more to his daily interaction with God, than the physical description of an action:

> *This is the account of Noah and his family. Noah was a righteous man, blameless among the people of his time, and he walked faithfully with God. (Gen. 6:9).*

Throughout the Old Testament we see examples of scripture in which walking is connected to relationship with God.

> *Walk in obedience to all that the LORD your God has commanded you, so that you may live and prosper and prolong your days in the land that you will possess. (Deut. 5:33).*

> *I will walk among you and be your God, and you will be my people. (Lev. 26:12).*

In the Hebraic mindset, walking is directly connected to how you conduct yourself, and how you live your life. This concept is not connected with the word for walk in any classical Greek writings other than the New Testament[9]. Therefore, while we have in our English Bibles a Great Commission that says

'Go!' Jesus was most likely saying 'as you walk your walk', or 'as you go about your daily life', make disciples.

For me this was a huge revelation, because this means that disciple making doesn't only apply to my friends who have been called on mission to Africa or Outer Mongolia! It applies to me day to day as I take my kids to their clubs, as I interact with the shopping assistants and as I dream with God for others.

Our daily walk should involve us being willing to see others through the eyes of God, ready to dream with Him for the sake of others.

Perhaps the biggest challenge when we open ourselves up to dream with God for others, is that there is a risk involved. I have had my heart broken and filled to overflowing in the same instant, when God has given me the smallest glimpse of how He sees the person I'm praying for. It can be overwhelming to the point of tears, and usually ends up with that person taking up permanent residence in my heart.

Sometimes we see things that are so wonderful we cannot contain ourselves. At other times we see hurt and brokenness in people that leaves us with no option but to weep with them, and assure them that God knows what they are walking through.

Yes there are risks, and yes it can be messy, but I have never had an experience of catching that glimpse of God's heart for someone else that hasn't had a positive result.

We may, at times, have insight into someone else's life and know it's not right to say anything. Rather we are to keep it in our heart and pray for that person. The positive side of this is that we are exercising our spiritual muscles, and keeping our gifts sharp!

Sometimes we see something or hear something of God's heart for another person and we need to share it. Providing it's within the guidelines and boundaries of a healthy, edifying and beneficial word, (my rule is simple: never give words about birth, death or marriage!) the person who receives it should be encouraged or provoked to pursue God. You, the giver of the word, can rest assured that God is using you, and that you are pouring your life out for others, fulfilling the command to love your neighbour as yourself.

Do you dare to ask God to show you what He sees?

If you do, and He does, you'll never be the same again…

Who am I
That You would use me?
Who am I
That You would speak through me?
I'm just a broken vessel,
Made whole by You.

All of my thoughts, I lay them down.
All of my plans, I put aside
Take my desires and give me Yours,
Give me Yours.

CHAPTER 7

The pain of unanswered prayer

Remember me,

Through the fire, through the valley

Remember me

Through the desert, speak to my heart

Of the plans You have for me,

And the ways You'll meet with me

In my tears.

The people of Israel roamed the desert for 40 years after disobeying God. During that time I'm sure they offered many, many prayers for an end to their 'temporary residency' in the desert. Was God not answering them? Did He not care? Had He forgotten the way?!

Their time in the desert was clearly not for any of the above reasons. This was a generation that didn't believe or trust in God, despite His grand rescue act in Egypt and the miracles He showed them along the way. This generation chose to grumble and pine for slavery instead of rejoicing in the freedom that was bought for them at the expense of countless Egyptian lives.

The long period of waiting came because the children of Israel had to be purified before God; the unbelieving generation had to physically pass away. Although it is difficult to grapple with, this is not a new theme in the Bible. Death and re-creation is a constant thread throughout each of the covenants. Because death has to come before new life.

Unanswered prayer could be called a trial, a desert experience, a test or sometimes a crisis. We have all experienced unanswered prayers at some point in our lives, and some are easier to deal with than others.

For me, one particular example of unanswered prayer is extremely painful. At the age of 11 I was diagnosed with scoliosis, curvature of the spine. I had two curves, giving me an 'S'-shaped spine. The result of this was a constant misalignment of my body, which in turn caused over-compensation in my hips, knees and ankles. Pain management became part of my daily life.

Worse than this, the misalignment of my joints put uneven pressure on the disks between my vertebrae, causing them to rupture frequently (sometimes called a slipped or herniated disk). This could happen through doing the most mundane things, like putting on my coat or rolling over in bed, and often left me bedridden or on crutches for weeks.

Throughout my teens and twenties, I continually sought prayer for this condition. Friends, acquaintances, family and those I'd never met before prophesied over me, speaking 'realignment', 'order' and many other wonderful prayers over my body. But my realignment never came. I battled with God over this continually, and all but lost hope for a miracle. I decided I would just have to learn to live with the condition.

Then, just a few years ago, I was in Jerusalem and met some friends who also felt led to pray over me. This time was different. I felt things moving in my back, the pain was disappearing and an indescribable heat flowed through my bones.

I could sense God was healing my back! My hips felt weird, because they were actually straight, and both sides of my waist actually matched each other. I was so excited I couldn't contain myself!

I was elated, and went through the next few weeks pinching myself in disbelief at the improvement. But then, just a few weeks later, the rug was pulled from underneath my feet. As quickly as the healing came, it disappeared. In just a moment, everything went back to how it had been before my friends prayed. I was back on crutches and bedridden with herniated disks again, and the misalignment in my joints had returned.

This was one of the hardest things I have ever had to deal with. I experienced the elation and joy in seeing years of unanswered prayers answered, only to have it stripped away almost immediately.

I couldn't understand it at all, and I became so angry with God. I almost felt offended, as if somehow I had earned the right to the healing I'd received, and I was being cheated of it. I had a sense of entitlement that I now see, with hindsight, wasn't right.

Who has the right to demand a body free from sickness or pain? I look at those born with disabilities, or who suffer far worse diseases and pain than I do, and I know I don't deserve my pain to be gone any more than they do.

Revelation 21 makes it clear that God's ultimate desire is for sickness and pain to be banished forever. Until that day we live in the period of 'now and not yet', where we see evidence of God's Kingdom ruling. So what we see and experience is a taste of what is to come – it is the Kingdom come in part, but not yet fully here. We see healing inexplicably happening sometimes but not always. All the while, Paul is also clear that God uses all things for 'the good of those who love him' (Rom. 8:28), even if we can't see, know or understand that it's for our good at the time.

Embracing desert times

The desert is a place of purification, confrontation, being set apart, restoration; a place for readying yourself.

During the Ascend ten-day programme that I help to lead, we take our participants out into the Judean desert for a morning and leave them there to seek and have an encounter with God in the wilderness. For many, this has proven to be the most impacting moment of the ten days. In the desert place they hear God most clearly, they receive revelation, they receive new songs, they see with clarity; they truly meet with God.

I have always loved the desert. I love the rugged land, the barrenness, the naked mountains, the striking shapes of the dried-up rivers and waterfalls. For me, the desert is stunning. So, when we ran our programme for the first time I was really excited to spend some time with God in the desert without having to chase after my three children.

I found a spot and sat myself down. Here's what happened:

I was sat on dry, hard, 'dead' ground, with two shrubs on either side of me, full of dancing, flitting butterflies. Ahead of me, I could see the mountains rising up imposingly, and behind me was the Dead Sea. Immediately in front of me was a worn, tired path, framed by a few pebbles, without which you would never have noticed the path was there.

Right in this spot God spoke to me clearly, in a way that I have not experienced before. In direct contrast to the feelings the Israelites must have felt during their 40-year walk, God showed me that He actually wants me to *stay* in the desert. There was life and transformation all around, but the desert place was for me. For now.

I have always been an 'off-the-beaten-track' sort of girl. There I was, off the path, in my little spot, with the glorious mountains ahead of me – my eyes fixed on the high places, bitter waters behind me. I was surrounded by life. But I was still in the desert.

This left me utterly undone. It all made sense to me for the first time in my life. I found myself praying that God would keep me in the desert: 'God would you keep me in the wilderness, I want to stay in a place of desperation for you, I want to stay in a place where you are my lifeline and my All in all.'

And then it hit me – my back was part of this. My pain, my discomfort, the fact that I never knew if and when I would be back on crutches or bedridden. This was all part of the desert where God has chosen me to be for now.

There is always purpose, there is always a use, nothing is ever wasted. Despite my kicking and screaming, despite my tears and the frustration of not being able to pick my kids up, despite my lack of understanding God still had a purpose.

He showed me that in the desert, this place of purification and utter dependence on Him, there is life, there are high places where you can see how far you've come, and can aim higher. There is also transformation.

Since then, I am learning to accept and embrace this desert season. (I do believe it's a season, and that there will be seasons for living in Eden too!). I am also learning not to fight Him when He leads me and keeps me in the desert. Perhaps unsurprisingly, the fruit that I have seen around me since this realisation has been much more abundant.

While I might be loathe to say it, and while it is a physical hindrance, the pain in my back serves as a constant reminder of this word He showed me in the desert. I may not enjoy the pain, but, even in the hardest moments, I can take joy that God has me here for a purpose.

Sometimes I laugh at how slow I am to realise the prayers I need to pray. But this was a big one for me – perhaps it will be for you too:

Do you dare to ask to stay in the desert and trust that He is there with you until His work is completed?

I look to You,
Maker of all things.
You know the depths of me
In my fears.

You will not let
My foot slip.
You watch over me
In my tears.

Remember me
In the fire, in the valley.
Remember me
In the desert, speak to my heart
Of the plans You have for me,
And the way You'll meet with me
In my tears.

CHAPTER 8

The desert cry

Speak tenderly to me,
Be patient in Your love.
Speak words of hope,
And free me,
You are making all things new.

When leading worship not long ago, my mind was drawn to the amazing story of Hosea and his wife, Gomer.

Theirs is a love story that actually dances between two stories; the human narrative about Hosea and his unfaithful wife, and its prophetic counterpart between God and Israel. The story has so many facets to it, and contains so many things to be learned.

Perhaps one of the most famous verses is found in Hosea 2: 'I am now going to allure her ... into the wilderness and speak tenderly to her' (v.14 in part).

There is so much contained in that one sentence.

The word 'allure' means 'to woo', to entice. It has romantic connotations, and indicates a deep and passionate love. Yet this is juxtaposed with the wilderness, which is a dry, difficult, desert place to be, a place with little or no physical refreshment to the body. Hot sun, dry heat, no water and dangerous conditions; it's not a place to get lost in! These words suggest that for some reason God wants to 'allure' us there.

Why?

The next verses in Hosea 2 tell of God's great plans for mercy, which will be given *in the desert place*. He wants us to be in a place with no distractions, with no ability to depend on ourselves, so that our gaze can't be taken off of Him.

Isn't it true that often it's only when we're in a difficult place that we can see Him plainly? It's only when there are no other noises that we can hear Him speaking to us. How He longs for us to hear those tender words of love and affection that He has been continually whispering to our hearts. If only we allow ourselves to be drawn to the place that is quiet enough to hear Him...

Being transformed

So what happens when we actually hear His whispers?

We are made new! From the beginning of time, God's words have brought forth life and creation. In Genesis 1, God spoke and the universe came into being. It is impossible to hear the tender voice of the King of the universe, the Maker of all things, the Messiah, Saviour and Lord of all without being changed.

When we see Him return, we will be changed in an instant. But we can begin the process now, if we'll only accept that alluring call into the difficult place of transformation.

How often do we, in a bid to protect ourselves, either go into the desert place kicking and screaming, or, even worse, do our best to avoid it altogether? But what happens when there is no one left to hear the complaints anymore, and nothing to remind us of what we left behind?

If we allow ourselves to look upward to the One who called us to this place, we end up forgetting what the fuss was all about, as we are drawn deeper into the true source of our joy.

The season in the desert is a *necessary* time of acute sharpening, a time of readying or training for the next season in our lives.

When we're in the desert, there are no pretenses and no excuses. We realise what priorities we've had, what our time has been spent on, what our thoughts have been occupied with and what has been influencing us. We realise all this because, all of a sudden, it's all gone.

We are confronted with the reality of our naked, unmasked lives. Sometimes it can be a shock to see what a masquerade our reality really has been.

When there are no other competing sounds we can suddenly hear the way we've been talking to others, notice the way we've been looking at others – and the way we've been hoping others will see us. Without life's usual filters, we have the chance to see how our standards have gradually slipped so far away from what God's standards for life are. It's only when we're in that place, when all has been taken away, that we realise that so much of what we held dear matters so little when held up against eternity.

In the desert, we are truly free to see.

It's in the desert that we can hear the words of hope, truth and love that God has been gently whispering for so long, yet the noise pollution in our lives has drowned out. In the silence, we can hear the words that set us free from all that bound us before, the words that make all things new within us. It's in the desert that we are most deeply refreshed, renewed and satisfied by Him.

I love how God turns the places that seem utterly lifeless in the natural into sources of life. He turns the places that we dread into the most incredible places of spiritual restoration.

'Therefore I am now going to allure her; I will lead her into the wilderness and speak tenderly to her' (Hos. 2:14). How many times have I read this verse, and left it there? Even when I have expected God to speak to me, I have neglected to read on. But there is more:

> *There I will give her back her vineyards, and will make the Valley of Achor a door of hope (v.15).*

We've been spoken to, allured and pursued by our Creator, lead into the desert. But then He promises to give us back our vineyards – this means that *we will be made fruitful.*

Think about it for a moment. He will call out to us, entice us, woo us and lead us into a place where there is *no* life. We'll be in a place where water is scarce and nothing can grow, and it's *right there* that He's chosen to give us back our vineyards! *Right there* is the place where He will bring life where there was none, fruit where we were barren and multiply what we thought had died.

This is the God of miracles. He takes us to a place of drought so that we can be in no doubt who our Source is. We can have no illusions about where this life is coming from, and who has made all things possible.

What about the Valley of Achor? What is this place?

A terrible thing occurred in the Valley of Achor. In the book of Joshua, we read:

> *Achan replied, 'It is true! I have sinned against the LORD, the God of Israel. This is what I have done: when I saw in the plunder a beautiful robe from Babylonia, two hundred shekels of silver and a bar of gold weighing fifty shekels, I coveted them and took them. They are hidden in the ground inside my tent, with the silver underneath.'*

> *So Joshua sent messengers, and they ran to the tent, and there it was, hidden in his tent, with the silver underneath. They took the things from the tent, brought them to Joshua and all the Israelites and spread them out before the LORD.*

> *Then Joshua, together with all Israel, took Achan son of Zerah, the silver, the robe, the gold bar, his sons and daughters, his cattle, donkeys and sheep,*

his tent and all that he had, to the Valley of Achor.
Joshua said, 'Why have you brought this trouble on
us? The LORD will bring trouble on you today.'

Then all Israel stoned him, and after they had
stoned the rest, they burned them. Over Achan
they heaped up a large pile of rocks, which remains
to this day. Then the LORD turned from his fierce
anger. Therefore that place has been called the
Valley of Achor ever since. (Josh. 7:20–26).

The Valley of Achor was a place where judgement was executed. Achor was a place where betrayal was dealt with, where an entire family was killed and where the anger of the Lord was appeased. This is the opposite of hope. This is a place of great sorrow, sadness and grief.

How are these two entirely different things connected? What do vineyards have to do with this painful valley of judgement?

I believe that it is in the wilderness, the place of utter dependence on God, that He can make all things new. He can and does bring fruit in a dry and parched place. He restores a place of tragedy to a place of hope, He turns all things around when we accept His pursuit of us, and turn our ear to His tender words.

And if new life wasn't quite enough, Hosea 2:15 isn't finished there:

Therefore, behold, I will allure her,
Will bring her into the wilderness,
And speak comfort to her.

I will give her her vineyards from there,
And the Valley of Achor as a door of hope;
She shall sing there,
As in the days of her youth,
As in the day when she came up from the land
of Egypt.

She will respond to Him as she did in response to her escape from slavery! What a moment of joyful exultation and singing that was. And here He promises that she will sing. And not just that - she will sing as she did in her youth. He will restore her youth!

That day while leading worship, I found myself deciding that when I notice the path I'm walking in life starts to get a little dusty, and a little more barren than I'd like, rather than dreading the upcoming desert season, I should count it a great privilege that God thinks I'm ready to learn something new.

It is a great honour that He has more things to prepare me for as it reveals to me that I'm not done, and He's not done with me. He has more treasures to speak tenderly to me, He has more fruit He wishes to see come forth from my life. I don't know about you, but with those results, plants or no plants, this desert sounds like the kind place that I intend of making the most of!

You call my name, I hear You
You beckon me, I follow.

You allure me to the wilderness,
Gently You win my heart.

Speak tenderly to me,
Be patient in Your love.
Speak words of hope,
And free me,
You are making all things new.

CHAPTER 9

Break me to make me

Made of clay
I pour myself out
I don't have the strength
So Lord I ask, won't You break me
I'm alabaster…

In Matthew 26 we read the story of the woman with the alabaster jar. Imagine the scene: there was a 'society dinner' being held at a Pharisee's house, with Jesus invited as one of the guests. The elite of the day sat reclined, merrily conversing around a table, when all of sudden in walked a scorned woman.

How awkward.

Heads turned, people stopped in their tracks, all eyes became focused on this woman, wondering how she got in and why she wasn't turned away at the door.

Then, in silence, this unclean woman made an utter spectacle of herself. The onlookers' embarrassment was tangible; their eyes filled with pity, yet, at the same time, utter disgust. They began to wonder: What on earth is she doing to his feet? When we will she stop so we can get on with their meal and forget this ever happened?

But Jesus did not stop her, He *saw* her, and she was not forgotten. This single act of passionate worship elevated her to a place of esteem. There could be no way she would have known the significance of this act, that it would be immortalised in the Scriptures. She would indeed, as Jesus said, be remembered through the generations.

This is an exceptionally beautiful part of her story that cannot be ignored. Yes, she was embraced and accepted by Jesus, but more than that – she was remembered. She was appreciated. Her act was commemorated. Why?

What did this woman do that was so important for us to remember?

Was it simply that she was accepted by Jesus when the religious leaders rejected her? Was it that she was tenacious enough to reach Jesus despite all of the obstacles in her way? Was it that she washed His feet with her tears? Was it because she saw something in Jesus that so many others had missed? It may be for all these reasons; each one is reason enough to remember her. This outrageous act of worship is packed with more than a few lessons.

Full of hope

In this particular story, the woman may well have been pushed, shoved and scorned; she was certainly viewed as inferior and as someone with less rights. Perhaps she had had to cover her head and most likely, her face, in order to get anywhere close to Jesus. Likely, she had to suffer comments, rude remarks and judgements at every turn she made. Yet she kept going, because she *had* to reach His feet. She had to weep, she had to give Him something.

King David was anointed on the head by a prophet , while *the Messiah* was anointed on the feet by a sinful woman.

This is one of the greatest pictures there is in the Bible. It gives us hope that *we* can interact with our Messiah too. And when we are before Him, it shows us *how* we should interact with our Messiah.

Interestingly this woman has no name; she is only known as 'the sinful woman' in Luke's account (Luke 7:36-49). Society did its best to tell her that she had no place or right to even be in the room. And yet Jesus allowed her into His presence, close enough to touch His feet. He saw her. He forgave her. He affirmed her right to be there. What an encouragement for us when we feel unworthy!

When given the chance to come before Him, the woman fell at His feet, undone by His presence. She had no words; she had nothing more precious to give than pouring herself out. She didn't hold back from extravagant expression, even though all those around her shamed her for doing something so seemingly foolish.

The woman smashed open her jar of perfume with reckless abandon, without a second thought, and poured it, unashamedly, on the feet of her Saviour. She didn't hesitate; she seemed as though she didn't care what she heard. All she wanted was to be completely abandoned to Him. She trusted that she would be accepted. She trusted that He would look through what was visible to truly see what others did not take the time to see; what was in her heart. Surely *He* would see in her what others had missed.

This is how we should be each day. There is a challenge for us in both the woman and the alabaster jar.

We can cast aside our guilt and shame and boldly approach His throne of grace, throwing ourselves at our Messiah's feet, knowing that He will accept us as we are.

Broken for a purpose

Once we are before Jesus we become like the jar of alabaster, smashed and poured out. We know that we have nothing to offer unless it's been made whole by Him. We sometimes don't even have the strength to ask Him to break us, but really that's the best prayer we can pray.

It's a dangerous prayer, because He'll do it. Being broken isn't easy, but it's truly the most beautiful thing He can do to us. What comes out of us when we are broken and poured out at His feet is a treasured and precious fragrance that pleases Him. He will see into us, like He saw into her, and He will remember us.

That is true worship.

Of course, we are not left broken as He doesn't leave things in pieces. Our God is a God of order, a God of restoration, a God who makes all things new. He is a God of new seasons, a

God of second (and more) chances, a God of compassion and love. We may well have to be broken, but it is only so that He can restore us and mould us into what He always intended for us to be.

He brings us back to what He purposed for us.

Sometimes we think that we can carry out DIY jobs on ourselves. We patch things up, thinking we're 'healed', only to find a little way down the road that it would have been far better to have been fixed by the One who made us originally. Because He knows us better than we know ourselves.

But by the time we get this far, the only way to be 'fixed' is to be broken and reset – like a bone that has healed in the wrong place. How comforting it is that our God is gentle, and will never break a bruised reed, or snuff out a smoldering flame (Isa. 42:3). He is a God of patience and tenderness. He will walk with us on this journey through brokenness, and carry us when we need Him to.

I heard You noticed
An unclean woman
And forgave her of her debt.
You called the sinner
Beautiful
I know my sins add up to more.

So I'll kneel

With my heart laid bare

With tears streaming down.

Made of clay

I pour myself out

I don't have the strength.

So Lord I ask, Won't You break me

I'm alabaster.

CHAPTER 10

Death and re-creation

You took my ashes and breathed life into the dust
You took my rags and gave me garments of praise.

The concept of being holy and pleasing in His sight is an ongoing, never-ending process. It's something that requires us to make choices every moment of every day. But, ultimately, it is about death and God's work of (re-)creation.

The Hebrew verb used in Genesis 1 for 'create' is 'Bara'. But this verb isn't used for creating with materials, like we as people do. We create a bowl out of clay, or a picture using paper and paints, whereas 'Bara' specifically means 'to create from nothing'. It's not a renewing or restoring process. It is about creating where nothing existed before. 'Bara' describes how God created the heavens and earth, from the 'formless' void.

As humans, we cannot create something out of thin air. We can only work with something we already have. Bara is something only God can do. In Psalm 51, David recognised this and cried out to God to *create* in him a pure heart (see v.10), not to fix one that was broken.

But why do we need a new heart? What's wrong with our old one? This is where death comes in.

The sinful woman in the last chapter stumbled onto one of God's greatest mysteries – that death must come before new life. We see this happen with the turning of the seasons each year. The trees die, the leaves fall, everything has to die in order for spring to come.

As the woman walked into that room to fall at Jesus' feet her pride was put to death, and, as the alabaster jar was smashed, her former life went with it.

Sometimes it isn't a specific act, like the sinful woman did, that causes us to 'die'. Sometimes it's about letting go of things we thought would live, whether that's people, dreams, visions, calls, friends or experiences.

For me, one such example was my thought that I would be involved in worship and music. I had to let that idea die a very slow and painful death, and be willing to let it go completely. I have seen this happen to many friends in many walks of life. It seems to be a tried and proven concept; that when we let our dream die, He can resurrect it in His time, in His way.

Sometimes it is something far more painful. Many of us have suffered mistreatment or abuse of varying kinds as children, or as adults. Sometimes our memories of these events are blurred and become clearer the further away from them we get, and sometimes they are too clear and we can't get rid of them.

For me, blurred memories of a past trauma became clear in a single moment, after many years. In that instant, I knew that if I was going to be completely free, I had to put to death my right to hold onto the identity of being a victim. For me to be truly resurrected into the life God has me, I had to let this part of me die, and, with it, any control that the particular situation had over me. It's not a simple or easy process, and neither is it easy or quick, but it is one that I believe is necessary for true life and freedom to be obtained.

Colossians 3 talks a lot about death: 'For you died, and your life is now hidden with Christ in God' (v.3). 'Put to death, therefore, whatever belongs to your earthly nature' (v.5).

Before we can choose life, we must willingly choose to die. Our 'self' has to be put to death. Jesus wasn't exaggerating when he said we have to 'take up our cross' (Matt. 16:24) – the ultimate sign of death. We have to choose to daily die, whatever the fight of the day is.

When we choose to take charge of our own lives, without making space for God, we're on a road leading to death anyway: 'There is a way that appears to be right, but in the end it leads to death' (Prov. 14:12).

In God's order, it is only when we willingly choose to give up our lives, to be poured out and broken, that our hearts can be 'created anew':

> *Very truly I tell you, unless a grain of wheat falls to the ground and dies, it remains only a single seed. But if it dies, it produces many seeds. Anyone who loves their life will lose it, while anyone who hates their life in this world will keep it for eternal life. (John 12:24).*

The sinful woman who walked into the Pharisee's house no longer existed as she was. Her sins were forgiven and she was given new life.

You clothed me in white
Took away all my shame.
Disappointment turned to dancing
You called me by name.
Chosen and called by You
Rejection to adoption.

You took my ashes and breathed life into the dust
You took my rags and gave me garments of praise.

CHAPTER 11

The art of palatial spring cleaning

There is space only for You
On the throne of my heart.
I long and yearn to sit at Your feet.
Just to be with You,
Just to stand in Your presence,
Just to see You in Your glory,
Just to hear Your voice
This is all my soul desires.

It is actually quite easy to pay God lip service. It is not hard to say that we love Him, we adore Him, we put no one else before Him, we worship Him, we serve Him and anything else that describes *how* we interact with Him. I have been challenged about *who*, or *what* is *truly* ruling from the throne room of my heart. Who or what is taking that space from, or sharing that space with, Him?

This challenge came in the form of food and exercise for me. After having three kids I was determined to take control of my body, to get fit, lose weight and live more healthily. I threw myself at it, working out daily. I tried many different eating programmes that left me rigidly following plans that had no 'give' to them. I thought I was enjoying it. It brought results. I got fit. I gained muscle tone. I smashed many personal goals, like running 5K. I did it! Right?

Wrong. While reaching what felt like my physical peak, I reached an all-time low emotionally. I realised that if I was going to maintain the weight loss and stick at the same fitness level I would to have to deny myself constantly, discipline myself relentlessly, without any leeway, for the rest of my life. That isn't living. That is slavery.

I was desperate – my physical appearance was something I'd struggled with since I was a child. So I cried out to God, and it suddenly dawned on me while in a real dark moment of desperation; I had never sought to hear what God's opinion was on this matter. I had tried to force through a solution in entirely human ways, without even considering that He might have His own way.

Over the next few days and weeks, I worked through the deep and painful realisation of how many things I had put things before Him. I lay on my floor and cried. I wrote pages and pages in my journal. I talked it through with a trusted friend, and I sat at my piano and poured out songs of freedom and repentance. I realised during that time that I had managed to make an idol from what was essentially a good intention and a 'right' desire – to be healthy and look after my body.

Through this process, I suddenly felt freedom for the first time in my life in this area. I came to understand that God has made a way for us to live healthily, without overly strict plans, obsessive calorie counting or restricting ourselves to never enjoy food again. A spiritual and emotional weight lifted off me, and guess what? I *did* lose weight physically, too!

The weight loss in my story isn't the point here, and I wouldn't want to give the impression that this whole area is completely resolved in my life, even now. However, I came to realise how many times I'd not run to God when I was feeling down – I'd run to a chocolate bar instead. It dawned on me that I'd put a piece of chocolate on the throne of my heart, rather than the Almighty Creator of heaven and earth. Chocolate!

Just when I thought I was taking control of my situation, I began to idolise other things in the place of food – my performance in my workouts, my achievements, the number of pounds lost. Just like food before it, this was where I was basing my sense of satisfaction on.

Finding comfort in the wrong place

Your idols may not have anything to do with food or exercise – they may be music, work, technology, money, pornography, friends, ministry, family, even 'spiritual highs'. It could literally be anything that you inadvertently place before God, so ask yourself: where do you run to when you want comfort?

It can be really hard to run to God when we need to the most, because sometimes in those moments He feels furthest away. Our culture is one of instant gratification, so instead of God, we look to a quick fix, and this becomes a crutch without us even knowing or noticing. Not only this, but we don't even realise how these temporary fixes gradually take over. They begin to come between us and God, and can even take His place completely. Sadly, while they may satisfy us for a few minutes or even hours, they can never deal with the root of our problem.

I discovered that the root of my problem was emotional – I had become a comfort eater, without even noticing. I had no idea how many times a day I ran to food instead of God, and I continued doing so until I found a strategy to distinguish between my heart needing to be fed, and my stomach needing to be fed. Up until this point I couldn't tell the difference, and used my self-made comforter for both – food. What an amazing experience it was to learn that there was a difference. I learned that I could feed my heart on God and my stomach on food – both in their rightful – and enjoyable, places.

I'm always challenged by the following statement my friend Sarah made: 'The final question presented to humanity is this: Who will you worship?'[10]. I know that I have worshipped food, fitness and the ideal of being thin and muscly, without even realising it.

The things that we use to feed our souls, the things that we believe will 'nourish' us, these are the very things that we worship. They may be good things, but they can never truly satisfy us fully or be the source of our joy or identity. God gave us such gifts to enjoy, but our enjoyment of them should always point to the source – Him.

If the joy and satisfaction that we draw from other things become even slightly too emphasised, or they become a crutch to help us gain even the smallest amount of our identity, then they've climbed up onto that throne and have taken the place of the King.

I'm not saying that we should deny who we are, as God made us. I am a mum, I am a friend, I have been given a family to enjoy. These all make up part of my identity, but none is the entire summation of who I am. Together (with many other things) they each make up the calling and role that God has for me. My identity, the true essence of who I am made to be, is wrapped up in Him.

During my own personal processing of this truth, I have become aware that God gently peels things away on purpose. He strips us back, getting rid of the 'stuff' we wrap ourselves in, because those are the things we have allowed to become ruling forces in our lives.

Stewarding our hearts

A few years ago our family was blessed, for the first (and possibly last) time, with the privilege of owning a new car. It was such a treat to drive something clean and new, with no spots and blemishes. It was actually upsetting the first time I noticed that someone had left a scrape across the bumper while I had been away!

We still try and clean our car once a month, both inside and out. It is remarkable to see how much dirt and grime builds up just through daily use.

The concept of 'keeping something new' or 'stewarding possessions' might be easy to grasp when we can see them physically in front of us, but how often do we consider how we steward the clean heart that has been created in us?

Our hearts are no different to our car; through the course of daily life the dirt and grime gets left as residue. If we are not careful, before long the junk starts to build up, and the throne of our hearts becomes filled with clutter, grime and junk.

If God has created new hearts within us, then we have a duty to live in purity, to keep our hearts clean. This is more than simply for the sake of feeling good. There is a direct connection between purity and authority.

When our hearts become cluttered and dusty, when we draw nourishment for our souls from idols instead of God, that authority is lost. Remember the story of Elijah in 1 Kings 18? The prophets of Baal learned the hard way that the idols they were literally worshipping were powerless. When we idolise things in our hearts, we are inadvertently expecting power to come from them, or at least elevating them to an equivalent position to God. With that, comes the death of purity and holiness.

When our clean heart is compromised, so is any spiritual authority
that we've been given. Hebrews 5:8–10 says:

> *Son though he was, he learned obedience from*
> *what he suffered and, once made perfect, he became*
> *the source of eternal salvation for all who obey him*
> *and was designated by God to be high priest in the*
> *order of Melchizedek.*

> *Once Jesus conquered death, He had the authority*
> *to set us free from our punishment, and was given*
> *a place at the right hand of God 'far above all rule*
> *and authority, power and dominion, and every*

*name that invoked, not only in the present age but
also in the one to come.'*
(Eph. 1:21).

That is the authority that comes with purity!

Now, while we know that we cannot obtain perfection, we have been purified through Jesus' death, and we can continue to walk in purity. We are in this world to represent Him, our pure God, to those around us. If we expect God to work through us, and He is pure, then we too must walk in purity. Spiritual authority comes as a pure people, representing a pure God, speak and act in assurance that God is with them.

Spiritual authority is the ability to give orders, make decisions and endorse obedience in the spiritual realm. That is a responsibility that anyone would be very careful to give, as it's so easily misused. The correlation between purity of heart and spiritual authority is therefore vital.

Just as a judge cannot do his job with authority if he has a criminal record, God isn't going to give the same amount of authority to someone who has filled their heart with things that are not of Him as He is to someone who has set their eyes on Him and has committed to having a heart after Him, like David (Acts 13:22). He needs to be sure that His people hear His voice, and share His heart, and only then can He give His authority to us, over situations on earth, as though He Himself was there.

When we allow our hearts to become cluttered, the process of emptying, ordering, stripping back and restoring gets harder and harder, more and more painful. But God will still take us through that process, if we let Him, because He is committed to having a pure and spotless bride (Eph. 5:27).

We have discovered that it's much easier to clean a car (or home) regularly than to wait several months. David had to walk through this process too, but God had the grace to bring the prophet, Nathan, into his life to speak the truth that led to confession from Psalm 51 that we read in the last chapter.

There will probably be things that have taken up residence in our hearts for decades. God wants us to be who He made us to be – without all the bolt-ons we add. He takes time to strip us back to our original design. Yes, He'll use all we've been through to teach us things, but so often we think we can outsmart God. We think we can out-design the ultimate Designer, or out-create the Creator, helping Him by adding things to the already perfect recipe. God didn't leave things out when we made us. He got it right – exactly right.

In dying to ourselves, we find life – a theme we see throughout the Bible. We have to trust that the King knows best.

There will be things in our lives that are hard to root out, but the King will take the time to do so because He wants a clear throne room. He longs for us to have no distractions, so He can speak and we can hear clearly. He wants us to be able to run to Him and not trip, so He can love us. He demands that nothing or no one else takes His place as our first love.

Do you dare to ask God to reveal what's in your throne room? Are you willing to clear it when He does? You may find unexpected things sitting on your throne – like I did – or you may already know what sits on your throne. In either case, the King is ready to be given back His throne. He's waiting for you to accept this challenge to gently re-order your throne room, and let Him take up permanent residence.

Would you make me,

Worthy to see You?
Hide me in the cleft of the rock
Pass before me,
In all of Your Glory
Would You show Yourself?

There is space only for You
On the throne of my heart.
I long and yearn to sit at Your feet.
Just to be with You,
Just to stand in Your presence,
Just to see You in Your glory,
Just to hear Your voice
This is all my soul desires.

You are a Holy God
You demand a Holy response.

CHAPTER 12

Your great rescue

Grace abounds

In waves so strong

I'm all out at sea

I'm right where I want to be

Grace abounds

Engulfing me all around

I'm all out at sea

Right where I want to be

Until You've done all You need in

Just me and You.

In Your great rescue.

Life is an ocean. It is full of twists, turns, and currents pulling you in every direction possible. It can get rough in an instant, but can also be so beautiful and refreshing at times too. The choppy and tumultuous times that life can throw at us can come even in the most sheltered and luxurious of lives. The currents can come from within just as much as from any external circumstance.

For some, the storm comes because circumstances around them amount to a storm that is somehow completely out of their control, and they struggle to stay afloat in all that is being thrown at them. We all know stories of people who lost their job, and then a parent passed away, and then they crashed their car, and, and, and…

The circumstances around them created the storm they found themselves in.

Then there are internal storms. As a teenager, I exemplified this perfectly. I battled with unhealthy eating habits, negative thoughts about how I looked and I also struggled with friendships. I was depressed one minute and elated the next; fighting and making up with friends just as quickly. But the storm that was hardest for me was the battle of food and weight. No one knew the struggle I had being surrounded by what I saw as 'perfection'. I flirted with multiple eating disorders and couldn't get out of the storm.

For others it could be the struggle of depression, or lust. There are many internal storms that engulf our minds.

Sometimes we're ready and waiting for the waves, because we know we're walking through a storm, or that one is coming. Perhaps it started with a light drizzle, the winds picked up and we were ready, with our coats, boots, umbrellas, ready to protect ourselves from any eventuality. Although we may not anticipate every wave that comes in, we are prepared to deal with them because we recognise the stormy times that we are living in.

Other times, we're happily enjoying a quiet, peaceful picnic for the soul, then, in an instant, we are being pounded with the lashing rain of a storm that arrived with no warning. We're not ready; we are stuck outside in our summer clothes getting soaked to the bone! Our picnic is ruined; our food has turned to a soggy mess and is no longer appetising or satisfying. The rain stings our skin and we can't see anything clearly, saturated by the storm before we've even had a chance to put our defenses in place.

What if God had a plan in the suddenness of the storm? What if He *meant* to 'catch you unaware'? What if He didn't want that food to satisfy you anymore? What if He has things He wants to do in you during the storm? What if He wants you to stop fighting the tides, and give all control over to His currents? Would you let Him carry you? Even if that means being all out at sea, with seemingly no hope, and no direction?

Saved within the storm

God knows that He gets a lot less done in us when we're ready and prepared to deal with all the things that are going 'wrong' around us ourselves. Before we take a moment to look up or consider who might be the author of the storm, we charge ahead to 'fix' His handiwork.

I believe that's why some storms come 'suddenly' and out of the blue. Because in His mercy He saves us from ourselves, from our incessant need to be in control and find the easy way out.

What if we're supposed to embrace the storm and all it brings, and *trust* that He's good?

He's always good.

His grace abounds, engulfs us, surrounds us, it carries us in His currents to the places He where wants us to be. If we stop fighting it, we might discover that we have been transformed, washed clean, renewed, restored and directed in ways we never could have accomplished for ourselves.

What if God isn't as interested in saving us from our circumstances as He is in saving us from ourselves? What if His plan is rather to save us *through* our circumstances?

What if God is leading us right into the eye of the storm, where *being* in the storm with Him *is* His great rescue plan?

Stop fighting

In this book, we have looked at the many different ways in which God draws us into places of complete dependency on Him. It could be in the desert, in a storm or in an olive press under great pressure (as we will see later). All of these seasons have one thing in common, and one goal. To further ready us for our destiny, and for eternity.

If we spend our life fighting against every method God may use to make us more like Him, then the trials and storms will only intensify. God doesn't give up on us. He has wonderful plans for His partnership with us, and, as long as we profess trust and commitment to Him, He will draw us to Himself by any means necessary. He will chase after us, longing for us to adore Him as much as He adores us. He will lead us and direct us into situations that can't be orchestrated, in order for us to learn more about who He is, and so that we can be transformed into His likeness.

The current's so strong
I'm swept away
In Your ocean so great.
I ebb and flow
In this great expanse
With no control, no control.

I've nothing left
To fight the tides
I want to be carried.

Grace abounds

In waves so strong

I'm all out at sea

I'm right where I want to be

Grace abounds

Engulfing me all around

I'm all out at sea

Right where I want to be

Until You've done all You need in

Just me and You.

In Your great rescue.

CHAPTER 13

Nothing can move me

Nothing can move me,
Nothing can move me,
Your joy came in the morning…
Your promise will keep me,
Your word it will lead me,
From death to life.

*I*n the previous chapter we looked at stopping the fight while in the storm. What happens though, then the storm is God's perfect way of making Himself known to you at this time? Maybe being sent into the eye of a storm *is* His great rescue...

Have you ever fallen into a fast-flowing river? I have.

When I was a kid I used to do water sports in the river that ran through the middle of the city I grew up in. One time, my wind sail caught a gust and took me out of the safe area in the dock into the main body of water where I immediately felt the strong pull of a massively powerful river.

I fell off my board almost immediately and began screaming for help. I realised instantly that although this huge river looked lazy and slow, it was powerful and swollen, and had the potential to suck me under and lose me in its depths. Fortunately for me, my coach was nearby and got to me before I got carried away.

I don't remember much of this episode because I was completely overtaken by fear, but I do clearly recollect the moment that my coach got hold of me and pulled me up onto the safety of the deck. I remember the sheer relief as it totally overwhelmed me. The deck was solid, immovable, safe, which helped me calm down.

I have been struck by how I could describe a particular experience God took me through in my personal life in exactly the same way. I felt like I'd been lifted out of a situation that I had no control over and which could have destroyed me. Just like in that body of water, the power that sucked at me could have dragged me under and lost me forever.

When I left for university, I was so excited to be doing something I was absolutely convinced God had told me do, and for which He had opened the door so clearly.

From the very first day, it was like there was a systematic attempt to de-rail, confuse and overwhelm me with fears, negativity and doubts. I went through situations that should have had an abundance of pastoral care, but none was given. I saw my faith deconstructed with no space for processing or reconstruction. Instead of being encouraged in my gifts and abilities, I was constantly torn down and my place there felt constantly questioned. The experience of being there was something that almost destroyed my faith, and it rocked my confidence in my gifts and my identity like nothing else ever has.

I completed my studies hanging by a thread in so many areas of my life. I left deeply saddened by so much of what I saw and experienced, and felt let down, betrayed and disappointed.

I didn't recognise how hard I had been screaming for help until I realised that God had rescued me! He heard the cry of my heart without the words ever needing to be uttered. He saw me, saw the danger and grabbed me before it carried me away completely.

Sometimes, we don't realise what God has rescued us from until we have the blessing of hindsight. We can reach the depths of despair, hit rock bottom, before God grabs us. Sometimes we need to know that we need Him, that we cannot save ourselves. I believe that is why we often reach 'rock bottom'. It's the moment we know for certain that we cannot do it without Him.

Rescue and realisation

We may all have different stories and experiences of God's incredible rescue acts, but one thing we all have in common is the immovable place that He carries us to when He rescues us.

He places us on a rock (Ps. 40:2) and gives us His peace and His rest. When we are there, nothing and no one can move us, even if they try to. This is His precious gift to us, and often we don't need to ask for it. He not only lifts us to a higher place, but He dries us off and washes us clean.

Moving from a chapter about stopping the fight, into one about being in the storm may be confusing, but this is a perfect example of this constant tightrope balance we walk, or resting and wrestling in our pursuit of God.

I've found through the rescues I've experienced that after that initial plucking from imminent danger, we can sometimes be plunged into a night of the soul. This is a time where nothing much happens, we're left alone with our thoughts, our prayers and our relief that the situation has changed. It's a time for deep healing, deep restoration and often painful realisations, but, after night time, always comes morning (Ps. 30:5).

After I completed my studies, I moved to a different city. I felt like I needed a long retreat to work through some of the ramifications of my time at college. I needed space, time and patience from all who were around me. God knew I also needed to succeed at something! I went to train as a teacher, and, through this year of hard study, it was like a retreat for my soul and my heart. I was around people who believed in me again. I was in a congregation that was happy to let me go through what I needed to. I was training in something I seemed to have a natural ability for too. During this time I slowly started healing and putting my faith back together again.

With the morning come new mercies. God knows what the soul can bear, what the mind can cope with and what the heart can carry. His mercies are *always* towards us; His mercies *always* triumph – and He *loves* to show His mercy. Even when we deserve to be swept away by that swirling current, He shows His mercy – because that's who He is.

It is only when we have a full realisation of His mercy that our morning can truly break. It is when we grasp this undeserved and unending mercy that joy can burst forth in our hearts. In *this* place, I have experienced the joy that wells from depths I didn't know existed, bubbling up from my deepest parts. This is the joy that He promised for us in our despair; this is the life that He spoke when we were still dead; the flourishing He saw when we were drowning.

From *this* place, nothing can move me.

I will rest here for a while

I will wait here for your rain to wash me clean.

I will sit here at Your feet

There's no other voice, I want to hear.

Nothing can move me,
Nothing can move me,
Your joy came in the morning...
Nothing can shake me,
Nothing can rob me,
Your joy came in the morning.
You promise will keep me.
You word, it will lead me
From death, to life.

CHAPTER 14

Fresh oil

Let the pressure be just right.
Let the darkness be fleeting and never lonely,
So that what comes forth is pure,
And an oil You're pleased with.

On a family day out, I had the privilege of seeing my son operate an ancient olive press. He followed the instructions given to him perfectly, and pressed a few olives so we could begin to see the oil seeping out of them.

This simple visual example of a biblical truth made the extent of the meaning of the olive press more real to me than ever. The struggle that each olive goes through to produce this precious oil is a clear representation of what God does with us. We need to be squeezed, refined and put under pressure in order for a pure offering to come out of us.

Do we dare to ask for that pressure? It's a dangerous prayer. It's a scary thing to be thrown into the olive press, we have to trust that the press won't crush us completely; that we will survive whatever ordeal we are going through. This trust has to be coupled with knowing that God loves us. He isn't out to crush us, He will not give us more than we can bear and He wants the best for us. We have to trust that the pressure we're subjected to is just right, even when we think, in our humanity, that it's too much.

When an olive is in a press it is not only subjected to pressure, but it's also surrounded by other olives, all of which are also being subjected to pressure, from different angles and at different times.

This is also true of our journey with God. We are never alone. Even if we rest assured that God is with us and doing a great thing in us through this pressure, we can take comfort, too, from the fact that others are going through their own press, their own journey, their own story.

Embracing the darkness

As that great olive grinder rolls around in its rut, there is a moment when it passes over the olives for the very first time, and the olives are plunged into complete darkness. This is the time of the most intense pressure, but it is also the time when the purest oil is produced.

I have been learning recently to embrace the times of darkness, of pressure and squeezing, trusting that this is God's beautiful way of getting the most pure and sacred offerings to come out of my heart.

Fit for a king

Olive trees are unique. They are easily recognisable by their thick trunks, growing wider with age, their silvery green leaves and, of course, their fruit. The fruit, when picked too early is bitter and hard, and not pleasant at all to eat. But when picked at the right time, olives are delicious and very good for the health.

An olive tree is virtually impossible to destroy. Even if a tree is set on fire, and razed to the ground, an olive tree will regenerate itself and bring back shoots from under the ground. Perhaps this is why the olive tree is the national emblem of Israel, a people who have routinely been persecuted to the point of being almost destroyed, and yet they have remained. More importantly, though, this may be why it was also used to make anointing oil.

In the Bible, God commanded the use of oil when ordaining a new king. In 1 Samuel 10, we read that the prophet Samuel anointed Saul, the first King of Israel, by pouring olive oil on his head. Olive oil used to signify the chosen one of God. I believe that there is something significant in the fact that olive oil was used. It comes from a tree that is almost indestructible, much like the promises that proceed from the mouth of God (Isa. 55:11). What better way to represent this than by using olive oil.

Finally, the olive tree is a symbol of peace. It was an olive twig that the dove brought back to Noah in Genesis 8:11. The fresh leaves in its beak were a symbol that the wait was over. The time of fruit was coming, and the time of being hidden away was ending.

This is not a commentary on the meaning of the olive tree, but rather an opportunity to draw from both nature and biblical imagery encouragement for the seasons of life we walk through.

In the press

Maybe you're in the olive press right now, and you're feeling the pressure and pain of the darkness and being moulded into a different shape.

My husband changed his job a couple of years ago, into a new role that required more international travel. I was very worried about this, as we had three small children all very close in age. He had worked at home up until this point, so it was a big change in dynamic. For me this was made even more complicated as I, too, had been given new responsibilities in ministry and work, and family life only worked when we 'shared the load' of childcare as a couple.

With my husband having to go away for extended trips more often, I felt I had been thrown into the olive press and was under immense pressure that I couldn't get out from under. It felt relentless and intense from morning to night, with no relief. I was managing my own work, all the children's schedules, the house, the cleaning, the cooking, shopping, laundry, play dates, clubs and a million other things (it felt like) on my own. I was ready for a melt down.

What happened actually surprised me. By the end of week two of a long trip, I realised that I had found a rhythm. I had found a supply of grace that I didn't know existed, and I had patience that I've never experienced before. I knew this was a 'pure oil' moment; the pressure and intensity had somehow managed to bring out so much good in me, good that I wasn't convinced was even there! It didn't make the situation any easier to deal with, but God somehow brought a surprisingly good product out of this bitter and hard olive as it got thrown into the press.

Be encouraged that pure oil will also come from you in this season, oil that is worthy to be poured out in order to proclaim His unchanging promises.

Maybe you're feeling like you've been utterly destroyed, burnt out, ruined by what life has thrown at you. Remember that even from a stump a shoot can come forth. It *can* bring forth fruit and hope.

Whatever circumstances we are walking through right now, we can be spurred on by the picture of the olive tree and its produce.

No one said it would be easy, but do we dare to ask for the process that brings about the most precious and pure of sacrifices?

Let there flow out from this press
The finest of oil
Ready to be poured out at Your feet.

May the pressure be enough
May the darkness be fleeting and never lonely,
So that what comes forth is pure,
And an oil You're pleased with.

Refine me, rid me of imperfections.
Take me out of the picture
So that all You see when You look at me
Is a reflection of You.

CHAPTER 15

An inheritance to fight for

I will wrestle, 'till the morning comes
Just to see Your face.
I will wrestle, as long as it takes,
To see You face to face.

We've already mentioned the story of Jacob wrestling with God (found in Gen. 32), in an earlier chapter. He did not give up or let go until God blessed him. It's a wonderful story of the tenacity of Jacob that teaches us so much about intercession, and about being willing to ask God for a blessing.

Psalm 24:6 says:

> *Who may ascend into the hill of the Lord?*
> *Or who may stand in His holy place?*
> *He who has clean hands and a pure heart,*
> *Who has not lifted up his soul to an idol,*
> *Nor sworn deceitfully.*
> *He shall receive blessing from the Lord,*
> *And righteousness from the God of his salvation.*
> *This is Jacob, the generation of those who seek Him,*
> *Who seek Your face. Selah*

Jacob became synonymous with this concept of wrestling, seeking, contending for more – so much so, that David includes this quality as part of his answer to the question of "Who may ascend the hill of the Lord".

The descendants of Jacob

Joshua is a book that includes the story of the Israelites finally taking possession of the Promised Land. There are mighty warriors, the fall of Jericho and many other miracles contained within it. But what I love most about the book of Joshua is its three unassuming stories of women who make outrageous requests and change history in the process.

We've already looked at Rahab, but there are two other instances of women in the book of Joshua who dared to ask for things and their tenacity was honoured.

Achsah: daring in her request

We read in Joshua 15:16–19:

> *And Caleb said, 'I will give my daughter Aksah*
> *in marriage to the man who attacks and captures*
> *Kiriath Sepher.' Othniel son of Kenaz, Caleb's*
> *brother, took it; so Caleb gave his daughter Aksah*
> *to him in marriage.*
>
> *One day when she came to Othniel, she urged him*
> *to ask her father for a field. When she got off her*
> *donkey, Caleb asked her, 'What can I do for you?'*
>
> *She replied, 'Do me a special favour. Since you*
> *have given me land in the Negev, give me also*
> *springs of water.' So Caleb gave her the upper and*
> *lower springs.*

Othniel, her new husband, was Caleb's nephew. Because of his bravery, he had won Achsah's hand in marriage, meaning that Caleb would not have received the expected bride price for her. Not only that, but Achsah then proceeds to ask for more!

We do not know if she was already married at the point of Othniel asking for the field, or if this was her first act as a betrothed woman, but clearly she was a strategic thinker. She knew that her father had the authority to give them land, to apportion to them some territory and she 'persuaded' her new husband to ask her father for a field, most likely as a part of her dowry. She must have known something about building and establishing a family estate, or legacy.

We see that she managed to advise her husband to ask for land, and he was given it. She must have been trusted and revered by her husband for him to listen to her on such matters, as it was not usual for women of this time to have a voice on such matters. Her role would normally have been restricted to the business of the home, kitchen and children. Not to land, and not to borders.

I love what happened next. Caleb, her father, was ready to grant Achsah her wish before she ever asked. He was an attentive father who saw she had a request and his desire was to grant it. As a betrothed woman, Achsah would have been considered married and therefore the responsibility of her husband. She no longer had the right to her father's property, and most certainly not to ask for land, which would mean her brothers would received less as their allotted territory!

Her father had already given her in marriage without payment, and also given her a field. This was therefore a *very* bold request, which she felt able to ask of her father.

It's the fact that she pushed passed the cultural boundaries of the day and approached him with boldness that made her request so unusual. The inheritance was evidently there for the taking, and she saw past the restrictions to boldly and directly ask: 'Give me a blessing; since you have given me land in the South, give me also springs of water' (Josh. 15:19).

We see echoes of Jacob's wrestle with God in her request, 'give me a blessing', as she did not give up until she got what she wanted. Achsah made a huge demand; she saw that she had been given land in the south, which is essentially desert land, with no water source. So she dared to ask for the springs.

Neither Jacob nor Achsah were content to just receive an inheritance, they both pushed, struggled and wrestled for the blessing.

This would have been hugely advantageous land to hold. It meant they would never suffer drought. Their livestock and crops would always be watered, and it meant they could provide for others in times of need.

But Achsah didn't just get the springs, she got both the lower and upper springs, which means she also got the source. She dared to ask not only for land, but the means to make it flourish and abundant. She asked for the source, the origins of the abundance, to be hers. That is tenacity!

The five daughters

The third instance is actually a set of five sisters: the daughters of Zelophehad. We read about them in Joshua 17: 3–6:

> *Now Zelophehad son of Hepher, the son of Gilead, the son of Makir, the son of Manasseh, had no sons but only daughters, whose names were Mahlah, Noah, Hoglah, Milkah and Tirzah. They went to Eleazar the priest, Joshua son of Nun, and the leaders and said, 'The Lord commanded Moses to give us an inheritance among our relatives.' So Joshua gave them an inheritance along with the brothers of their father, according to the Lord's command. Manasseh's share consisted of ten tracts of land besides Gilead and Bashan east of the Jordan, because the daughters of the tribe of Manasseh received an inheritance among the sons. The land of Gilead belonged to the rest of the descendants of Manasseh.*

Here we have the story of the lineage of Manasseh, accumulating in the births of five daughters and no sons to

Zelophehad. Daughters did not receive inheritance in those days; they married *into* inheritance. There was therefore no future guaranteed to a daughter outside of marriage and children. Their father was most likely heartbroken, realising his family line would end with him. But Zelophehad's daughters were no ordinary girls; they decided to fight for his lineage – the continuation of the tribe.

They fought for an inheritance, and to be considered as brothers, and they were granted their request. Here we see again that the inheritance was available to be claimed, but the cultural rules of the day forbade them from receiving it. They chose to fight for the right to be seen as equals, and, for a moment in history, they were deemed worthy enough to be given what should not have been rightfully theirs. As a result, their family name was preserved for generations to come. They made an outrageous request, and received what no women had previously received. Simply because they dared to ask…

Legacy and honour

From these three stories of women in the Bible we can see that legacy and honour always go hand in hand. You cannot leave a legacy if you function in dishonour. It's a principle we see throughout scriptures. Rahab professed that the God of the Israelites was the one true God, and she wished to be grafted into the people and their ways. She honoured the God of Israel and their laws and ways.

By contrast we read in Joshua 9 about the Gibeonites. They tricked Joshua into making a covenant of peace with them, and saved themselves from certain death in the process. It could be read that they did a brave and tenacious thing here, but I would suggest that there is a difference between tenacity and deception. The Gibeonites did not ever profess faith in the God of the Israelites. They did not join with the people, or become grafted into the promises of the God. They deceived the Israelites by using their ways against them. They knew that the law and the God of the Israelites placed the highest of values on covenant, and that covenants were binding. So they knew if the Israelites made a covenant with them, they would be saved and it would be binding.

In the case of Rahab, her tenacity resulted in a wonderful legacy of restoration, redemption and, eventually, the birth of the Messiah. For the Gibeonites, their deception led to their people being effectively enslaved for the rest of their existence. There cannot be a legacy without honour.

I believe this is a principle that has been so cheapened in the Church in many areas of the world. We rarely see true honour being given to those who have gone before us, and, sadly, we see a lot of self promotion and inflated egos.

I have been blown away to see how easy it is to honour those who have gone before us and to acknowledge how God has used them in our own lives, rather than just taking all the praise onto ourselves. I believe that God entrusts a bountiful legacy to those who are willing to live a life of honour in this way.

Rahab was a woman who dared to ask for freedom, and in the process of receiving that freedom, found restoration, redemption and honour.

Achsah, a woman who dared to ask for a blessing beyond her inheritance, who guided her husband with wisdom, and found abundance.

Mahlah, Noah, Hoglah, Milcah and Tirzah, the sisters who dared to ask for an inheritance they should never have been able to have, found a future and a legacy which extended for generations to come.

I will wrestle, 'till the morning comes
Just to see Your face.
I will wrestle, as long as it takes,
To see You face to face.

Give me Your blessing
Consume all of me.
Let me climb the ladder to Your glory
Mark me so I'll never be the same.

Final note

There are times when the world does a great job of robbing us of our dreams, of our joy and of our essence. We conform so easily to what we believe we're supposed to be, without giving a second thought to all the doubts our hearts might be voicing.

I would challenge you to listen to what is stirring in your heart. Maybe God is drawing you back to His original plan for you; maybe He's orchestrated things around you to be *this* hard because He wants you to change direction. Maybe He wants you exactly where you are, but you're thinking of moving on. Dare to ask Him to lead you to your own unique path.

When I finished my first draft of this book, I asked my husband to take a look over it. He told me that I should take some time to really soak in each chapter, and make sure I've truly captured the heart of what I wanted to say. I told him I didn't need to, since my whole life has been one long marinade in these principles!

Well, it turns out that God thought the same as my husband, and the process of writing this book has been like I've walked through the pages I've written, in real time. Even now, as I write this final note, I am lying horizontally on my sofa, with my back in agony again. This time my doctor has informed me that it may be something far more serious than

I have previously had, given that I have lost sensation and muscle strength in one of my legs. I am here, waiting for my MRI appointment while editing these final drafts, facing the reality of my own words and having to preach them to myself yet again.

I have to admit it makes me giggle; the irony of writing about the lessons of unanswered prayers and living with pain. It stands to reason that I should have to write this from a position of weakness and have what I've written and what I've claimed to have learned, tested, even up to the last minute! As I said earlier, I cannot 'preach' something that I am not willing to go through myself.

What I have written is not a series of magical formulas that make for a happy life, or a set of rules that provide a trouble-free existence. This book is an honest narrative of lessons learned the hard way, which have released me into rethinking the difficult circumstances of life as opportunities for growth, rather than things that have gone wrong. I have come to view the desert season and struggles as an honour and privilege that God would have more for me to learn, rather than thinking of it as a punishment or that I've been abandoned.

> *Ask the LORD your God for a sign, whether in the deepest depths or in the highest heights' (Isa. 7:11).*

> *Take delight in the LORD,*
> *and he will give you the desires of your heart.*
> *Commit your way to the LORD;*
> *trust in him and he will do this:*
> *he will make your righteous reward shine like*
> *the dawn,*

your vindication like the noonday sun.
Be still before the Lord
and wait patiently for him (Ps. 37:4–7).

God has so much He wants to give us – if we would only ask. He has joy, if we'd only ask. Sometimes God simply wants us to stop thinking with a sense of entitlement in regards to what we believe life should be like for us. He has favour, He has abundance in the desert places, legacy in the struggles and inheritance in the wrestling. He has fruit, blessings and influence that He wants us to walk in. He has authority, anointing, gifts and discernment, if we'd only...

Dare to Ask.

Acknowledgements

First and foremost, thanks be to God. What a surprise this project turned out to be! I expected that 'Dare to Ask' would be an album, a group of songs that I'd written, and the 'Dare to Ask' blog was simply my own personal chronicling of the process these songs went through. I never expected for the blog to turn into this adventure. Thank you God for the inspiration, the downloads, the beautiful moments of sharing your heart with mine.

Thank you to my amazing husband, who did so much in the proofreading and editing process and is undoubtedly my rock and best friend. #BestHusbandAward.

Thank you to my three amazing children, without whom I'm sure I would have forgotten how to laugh, and would not have nearly as interesting a life as you bring me. I love you more than words can say and I hope you grow up with the courage to ask for all that you carry in your hearts.

To my family; my wonderful parents, brother and sister-in-law (and Jesse) – thank you for the unshakeable friendships, support and love from all of you. I couldn't ask for a more fantastic family and a more wonderful upbringing. It is only because of your godly parenting that any of this could come to pass. To my mother-in-law, thank you for all your editing help, and for the ongoing support.

Thank you to Sarah and Andrey for your advice, your friendship and for being such fantastic colleagues and team mates. I am blessed beyond words to be able to walk beside you both. Thanks to Sarah for all the investment you have made into my life and for constantly calling me higher. Thank you for your encouragement, your friendship and for your beautiful Foreword.

Thank you to Michael, Steve, David, for your humbling endorsements and all the suggestions and edits you made along the way. I am so touched and thankful that you gave your time so freely in helping me with this project.

Thank you to David and Karen, to Rita and Peter, to Dani and LuAnne and all our family here in Israel. I am blessed beyond words to have such inspiring, wonderful friends and co-labourers around me.

Endnotes

1. John Bevere, Driven by Eternity: https://www.youtube.com/watch?v=S9X62XcSEN8 (accessed Jan 2017).

2. https://brimmingover.net/2017/01/21/iterate/ – taken from Andrew's daily email blast.

3. Ascend programmes are designed for anyone who loves to worship the Lord to access His presence, encounter Him and be transformed through worship, touring, teaching and workshops in the land of Israel. For more information see: **www.ascend-carmel.com** .
Details of the people involved in exchanges like this are kept confidential.

4. https://jwa.org/encyclopedia/article/rahab-midrash-and-aggadah

5. https://www.biblegateway.com/resources/all-women-bible/Rahab

6. A Yiddish word meaning 'shameless audacity, impudence'. https://en.wikipedia.org/wiki/Chutzpah

7. Her actual words can be read in Esther 4:11.

8. Robert Stearns, *The Cry of Mordecai*, (Destiny Image Publishers, 2009), used with permission.

9. Gunther Ebel, 'peripatevw' [peripateo; go about, walk] in *The New International Dictionary of New Testament Theology*, gen. ed. Colin Brown (Grand Rapids: Zondervan, 1986, p.943).

10. Sarah Liberman.

Made in the USA
Columbia, SC
24 November 2017